THE DIY INTERNET RADIO COOKBOOK

THE DIY INTERNET RADIO COOKBOOK

A BEGINNER'S GUIDE TO BUILDING YOUR OWN 24/7 STREAMING RADIO NETWORK

TOM TENNEY

Contents

Introduction   7

Chapter 1: Starting Out – Seven Important Questions To Ask Yourself   12

Chapter 2: First Things First – Finding A Streaming Host   21

Chapter 3: Getting Set Up – Building A Studio   31

Chapter 4: Unleashing Your Signal – Broadcasting Software   44

Chapter 5: Putting It All Together – DIY Automation   48

Chapter 6: Creating A Presence – Your Station's Website   77

Chapter 7: Life After Airtime – Distributing Your Content   108

Chapter 8: Necessary Evils – Music Licensing   124

Chapter 9: Strutting Your Stuff – Promoting Your Radio Station   133

Appendix: Resources   148

Introduction

It's no secret that the way we consume media has changed dramatically over the past 20 years, and radio has undergone perhaps more change than any other single medium. The way it is created, delivered and consumed has experienced paradigm-changing shifts, one of which is that it's now possible for anyone to create quality programming and make it available to a global audience. Gone are the days when it took an exorbitant amount of capital to purchase expensive professional broadcasting equipment, get licensed by the FCC, hire a staff of radio professionals to run the operation and a sales team to sell advertising to keep the venture solvent

Today, streaming radio on the Internet has allowed the independent media producer to do an end-run around FCC licensing, and digital technologies provide producers with all the tools they need to create a fully-functional radio station, complete with automation protocols. Of course, there are still legal concerns to consider - like music licensing to ensure you're not violating copyright laws with your broadcasts - but overall, the prospect of starting a streaming station with tens of thousands of listeners is well within reach of any ambitious independent radio producer with a basic knowledge of web technologies.

Before we jump in, I want to be very clear that I didn't start out as an expert on any of this - and to a large degree, I'm still not. I was the person that I imagine you are, someone with the drive to create great programming for my community and make it available to a worldwide audience. My problem was that I didn't have a lot of money to spend, so I needed to find a way to create it on a shoestring. Surely, I thought, there must be a book or a manual I can buy to guide me through the process, but there just didn't seem to be much out there. No books on Amazon, no convenient "How to Set Up a 24/7 Streaming Internet Station" how-to websites, no podcasts - nothing. I spent many late nights Googling up a storm and finally realized that, barring professional automation equipment that can cost a fortune, I'd have to get a bit creative and use what *was* available to cobble together something that did what I needed it to do. For three months I experimented, trying lots of things and failing at most, but in the end I was able to use technologies that were either free or very inexpensive to set up a system that would be able to handle around-the-clock programming and allow our hosts to easily create content, both live and pre-programmed. The goal of this book is to save you those hundreds of hours of blood, sweat and tears, the late nights experimenting with solutions and failing over and over again, and provide you with the tools that I wish had been available to me while I was building my station.

The book is arranged in what I consider to be a "logical" order, meaning that the chapters come in the order that I think you'll need them. Inside, you'll find tips and solutions for:

- Goal setting - In order to have a successful operation of any kind or size, it's important to understand exactly what you're trying to accomplish. Understanding this early on will be a huge help in determining how to build your radio station.

- Finding a company to host your audio streams, so your computer and Internet connection are relieved of the heavy lifting. I think you'll be surprised at how low a price you can pay for quality audio streaming.

- Creating a studio and obtaining the necessary hardware. Whether you're broadcasting from your living room or have a designated studio space, you will need some basic hardware to get the job done. At the bare minimum, you'll need a microphone, a computer, and an Internet connection, and I'll provide you with guidance on how to set these up for broadcasting. If you're looking to set up a fully equipped studio space, you may wish to add mixer boards, guest microphones, CD players, turntables or other equipment. I'll give you advice on the types of equipment you might need, as well as how to find them without spending a fortune.

- Broadcasting software: In order to get your signal out to the world, you'll also need designated software for encoding your signal into the correct format for your server, and sending that signal out to the world. This chapter will cover available options - some free, others very inexpensive - for reliable broadcasting.

- Your station's website: Any Internet radio station needs a website, not only as a destination for online listening, but as a way to promote your programming and distribute your content. This chapter will be a case study of my station's website, and will hopefully provide you with some good ideas for yours as well.

- Automation: This is the most difficult aspect for the net radio entrepreneur on a shoestring, but don't despair! There ARE ways to create a fully functional automation system on a shoestring, and one that will work not only with your streaming content, but for automatically updating your website as well. In this chapter I'll share the tools I used to do just that.

- Music licensing: The difficult reality of any radio station that broadcasts music is that, in order to stay compliant with the law, you must pay licensing fees for the music you play. This doesn't have to be a bank-breaking prospect, however, so in this chapter I'll provide advice on staying legal without going broke.

- Distributing your content: One of the great things about broadcasting in the 21st century is that your content can have a long life after its original broadcast. There are literally dozens of ways to get your radio content "out there" using your website, iTunes radio, radio apps, and by partnering with audio-content third party sites. This chapter will provide you with some tools to make sure your content continues to get listeners long after it first airs.

- Promoting your station: Any Internet radio station needs listeners in order to become successful. This chapter will provide you with some DIY strategies to promote your station and make sure listeners around the world are tuning in to your shows.

- Appendix - Resources: Finally, a comprehensive appendix at the end of the book will provide links to all the resources mentioned one place, for easy reference.

Please bear in mind as you go through this book that the solutions presented here worked for me to meet my goals, but may require some adjusting for your particular situation. For example, I work exclusively with Macintosh computers so some of the software I use may not work if you use only PCs. However, I've found that any piece of software that is platform-specific usually has a counterpart for alternative platforms. Wherever possible, I will provide links to several potentially useful solutions, and hopefully you will find one or more of them useful.

This book, like my radio station - Radio Free Brooklyn (RFB) - is a labor of love. It is designed to help the independent radio producer on a limited budget with a way to get something up and running fairly quickly. However, we all know how quickly technologies can change, so I invite you to sign up for updates to this book at my website: http://www.radiocookbook.com. Signing up with your email address will allow me to contact you when there are new developments affecting this book's content, and to give you the first look at new chapters that may be added before they go to print.

Should you have any questions about anything in this book - or suggestions on how to make it better - please feel free to email me at any time. My email address is tom@radiofreebrooklyn.com and I'd be happy to give you any help you need to get your station off the ground. I hope you find the help you're looking for within these pages. Best of luck to you and your Internet radio venture!

Chapter 1

Starting Out – Seven Important Questions To Ask Yourself

Before undertaking the task of building an online radio station, one of the most important preparatory steps you can take is *establishing goals* for your network. Doing this early will be a huge help as you're building your station and making decisions about what tools you need and how much to spend. With each decision you make along the way, asking yourself *"will this help me achieve my goals for the station?"* allows you to choose a strategy/tool/protocol that is the best one for getting to where you want to be.

In my two decades working in digital media, I've seen too many people embark on building a website or online community simply because websites or communities seemed to be popular, but without giving much thought to how it would serve their brand. Before you start building your radio station, you need to realize that it's hard work, and ask yourself some key questions about why, exactly, you're doing this. Some of the questions you should ask yourself are:

Question 1: What is it you're actually trying to accomplish?

Is your goal artistic expression, or is your main objective to make money? These two goals are not mutually exclusive, but understanding where you place your priorities will be of great assistance when deciding how you build your station.

Question 2: How much programming would you like to provide when you launch your station?

Do you want a station that only broadcasts a few shows a week, or do you want one that broadcasts around the clock, 24 hours a day, 7 days a week? Answering this question will help you to determine exactly how much automation you'll need to have when you launch.

Question 3: What's the format of your station?

The concept of *programming formats* is almost as old as radio itself. Simply put, it describes the kind of content your station will provide. Some of the most common radio formats include:

- News/Talk
- Classic Rock
- Country Music
- Adult Contemporary (music targeted to adults over 30)
- Electronic Dance Music
- Religious programming
- Urban/Hip-Hop
- World Music
- Freeform

At RFB, we decided to adopt the *freeform* format, which was pioneered in the 1970s by radio hosts like Steve Post and stations like New Jersey's WFMU and New York's WBAI. In a nutshell, freeform means that the station doesn't have an "official" format to which hosts and DJs must adhere. Instead, the hosts are given a time slot with which they can do whatever they like (within reason, of course.) Both my partner and I have backgrounds in running live performance spaces in NYC, and assign great value to giving artists free rein to create according to their own individual aesthetic. As a result of our decision to go freeform, we have a station with an eclectic mix of music, comedy, talk, and even a live sports show that takes calls from listeners. We realize that freeform is not for everyone - in fact, one if its downsides is that it's *not* for everyone, and someone listening to their favorite show on our station may not like the following show, and may tune out. However, having decided early in the process that we didn't want to place format restrictions on our hosts, and to give priority to artistic expression, this is a pitfall that we're willing to accept.

Question 4: Will you broadcast live shows, pre-programmed shows, or a combination of both?

Clearly, this is an important question to answer as the tools you'll need will differ depending on whether your shows are live or pre-programmed. There's nothing like live radio, and having live shows is likely to attract more listeners. It also provides more opportunity for community involvement, as it's fairly simple to set up your studio to accept live call-ins. However, live broadcasts require things like a place to broadcast from, live broadcasting equipment, and a layer of management over your studio facilities and your hosts that you will have to deal to a lesser degree if you simply air pre-programmed shows.

Question 5: Will your station make money, or is it exclusively a "labor of love?"

One of the most difficult challenges for anyone launching a media venture of any kind is determining how to keep that venture financially sustainable. Since this book focuses on building your station, and one could fill an entire book on moneymaking strategies (in fact, many have, and I list some of these books in the "Resources" section at the end of the book), I won't delve too deeply into this aspect of the station. Nonetheless, it's still an important question to consider. At RFB, we've made it a priority to keep the station "commercial-free," meaning that we don't sell advertising to just anyone who wants to buy airtime on our network. Instead, we rely on ancillary strategies to bring money in. Some of these include:

- **Live events.** This is a great opportunity, particularly for music-oriented radio stations. At RFB, we plan on hosting quarterly music showcases in our home neighborhood of Bushwick and in other neighborhoods around the borough of Brooklyn. Normally, bars with stages and sound systems can be procured in exchange for a guarantee that the bar will bring in a certain amount of money in gross receipts. Provided you're confident that you can bring in the audiences, this can be a great deal for producers since you can charge a cover fee and keep everything you earn at the door. Furthermore, it's fairly simple matter to bring along a laptop and a small mixer board and set up a broadcasting station so you can broadcast the event live to your listeners. Selecting bands with large followings will help bring people in the door, and if you're willing to offer your bands a percentage of the door based on who comes to see them, the musicians are further incentivized to encourage their fans to attend the show.

- **Donations:** This is a fairly straightforward strategy, but one that won't necessarily bring the big bucks, at least not right away. However, it's still worth it to have a place on your website for listeners to donate to your station if they like what they hear and want to contribute to the cause.

One way that we incentive listeners to donate to RFB is to offer premiums to those who offer recurring donations. For example, if a listener pledges to donate $5 per month - an amount that most people won't even notice when it's deducted from their bank account - they receive a free t-shirt. At $5 per month, the t-shirt is paid for after a couple of months, and everything on top of that is gravy. Five dollars a month may seem like small beans, but if you get just 20 people contributing that amount, you're looking at $100 per month - enough to pay for a significant portion of your operation.

- **Merchandise**. One of the truly beautiful things about this digital, on-demand age in which we live is that you don't have to lay out a huge amount of money up front in order to offer custom products to your listeners. At RFB, we were able to integrate our online store (which sells t-shirts, tank tops, tote bags, sweatshirts and mugs) with a company in California that receives orders directly from our store, prints the items and fulfills them for us - all at a very reasonable price. By doing this, we don't have to worry about things like managing inventory, upfront printing costs for items that may or may not sell, sending things out, or dealing with any fulfillment issues - it's all handled for us! Additionally, the company we use, Printful (described in more detail in Chapter 9), has such reasonable prices that we're able to mark up our merchandise so that we make at least $5-12 for every sale. We've also found that merchandise tends to sell very well at live events, and when we have an event we'll order enough merchandise from the vendor, at our discounted rate, in order to have inventory on hand at the event.

- **Live broadcasting for other organizations.** One of the great things about having your own Internet radio station is that you have a means of communicating with large amounts of people at a time - which is something that most organizations *don't* have. This can be used to your advantage, and is a way to potentially bring money into your network. Let's say, for example, that a local bar is having a music event that they would like to have broadcast to the world. As I mentioned in the "Live events" bullet above, it's a fairly easy matter for you to bring in some basic equipment to a bar with a sound system and get set up to broadcast remotely from the event. Not only is this a service that the event's organizers will pay you for, it's also great for your station as it will bring awareness of your network to perhaps thousands of people who may not have heard of you. You get paid, the organization gets their event blasted to listeners around the world, and you reap further benefits in increased listenership. It's win/win all around.

- **Media partnerships.** If you're fortunate enough to live in a large urban area, there will be a myriad of festivals and other cultural events happening in your city at any given time. Why not contact some of the organizers of these events and propose a partnership wherein your station will either live broadcast some of their events or, at the very least, have artists from their events appear on your station for interviews promoting the event? This is an offer that most cultural institutions, particularly the smaller ones, will find difficult to refuse. When starting out with this strategy, it's best not to ask for money, but to instead enter into a mutually beneficial relationship in which they agree to plaster your station's logo all over their programs, posters, and other promotional materials, and you agree to promote and/or broadcast their event. At the very least, this will gain your station some much-needed exposure, and after you've got a few smaller events under your belt, you'll be well-positioned to go after larger, national events who will be willing to pay for such partnerships.

- **Audio and podcast services**. Even if you didn't start out as an audio professional, starting and running an Internet radio station will allow you to develop skills in producing audio that most people, other than professional audio engineers, don't have. One revenue stream we've developed at RFB is offering audio production and post-production services to individuals and organizations that are seeking to develop their own audio content. Since NPR launched its *Serial* podcast in 2014, podcasting has experienced an explosion of popularity and more and more people are trying to get into the game. If you've got your own studio and equipment, why not offer to rent them out to those who might not have the same resources? At RFB, we offer services that range from podcast recording, to post-production (editing) and distribution at rates starting at $50 per hour. We advertise these services on our website, and for free using Craigslist.

Question 6: What will you call your station?

This may seem like a trivial matter, but believe me, the name of your station can and will be one of its most important assets and it's best to start considering this question early. A great name won't ensure success, nor will a terrible one guarantee failure, but considering that the name is the very first impression most people will have of your station, try to create something that resonates with them. Serendipitously, as I write this, I just got a *New York*

Times news alert that Google is restructuring its organization under a parent company called Alphabet. According to the article, Google co-founder Larry Page said, "We liked the name Alphabet because it means a collection of letters that represent language, one of humanity's most important innovations, and is the core of how we index with Google search." Clearly, Google put a lot of thought and consideration into the choice of their name, and chose one that is not only memorable, but that resonates with the core of who they are as a company. We chose the name Radio Free Brooklyn because we felt it would strike a chord with listeners on a number of levels, such as a) community - having Brooklyn in the name communicates that we are a Brooklyn-centric community organization; b) history - Radio Free Brooklyn has echoes of historic radio stations such as *Radio Free Europe*, which was created in 1949 as a way to broadcast messages of freedom into totalitarian regimes. This historic connection also reflects who we are in that we see ourselves as representing a "counterculture" of media artists who are struggling for artistic freedom in a media landscape that is increasingly governed by corporate interests; and c) utility - it's got "radio" right there in the name so there should be no question about what it is we do.

Question 7: What makes my station different?

There are literally thousands of Internet radio stations currently broadcasting, and more are added every day. While streaming audio is still a relatively young technology, the costs of getting your own station up and running have dropped dramatically in the past few years, and your competition is growing with each passing day. Perhaps the most important question to ask yourself before you get started is: what will make me stand out? To answer this question, you may wish to revisit question one: what are you trying to accomplish? It may be that you want to bring live, call-in radio shows about cooking and food to the Internet, or Cajun music to your community. The point is that you should be filling a need that is currently not being met, or telling a story that has not yet been heard. Even if your format is 24/7 Electronic Dance Music, think about ways that you can make *your* EDM station different from all the others. You'll be competing with thousands of voices, so make yours unique.

As should now be evident, there are a number of questions you should answer for yourself before you embark on the adventure of building your radio station. They're not easy questions - but important ones. I realize the impulse will be to get started on building your station right away, but if you take your time and consider each of these questions seriously and answer them as honestly and completely as you can, you will be that much better equipped to build what could be a wildly successful Internet radio enterprise.

Chapter 2

First Things First – Finding A Streaming Host

It may seem to you that procuring a streaming server host would be one of the *last* things you'd want to do, right? After all, there's so much work to do before you're ready to start streaming your station out to the world, so why not save that step until the end? However, since the choice of streaming provider is one of the most important decisions you will make - you want to choose a reliable host that offers quality service and support - I always recommend that anyone building an online radio station considers hosting options as early as possible. Case in point: most providers advertise a guaranteed uptime of over 99.9%, but how will you know if that claim holds true unless you do your own testing over a significant period of time? How will you know anything about the quality of the stream unless you've tested it thoroughly before you launch your network? It's much easier to test out streams, and change providers if needed, *before* you have programming going out over that stream to hundreds or even thousands of listeners. Additionally, some providers offer free trials, usually for about a week, but only allow a few listeners during the trial period. For these reasons, I strongly recommend that you begin shopping for a streaming solution that works for you as early as you can in the process.

What a streaming host provides, and why you need one

Before we dig in to selecting a host, I should probably briefly explain what a streaming host does, and why you need one. Back in the late 1990's, when Internet audio and video first arrived on the scene, listening and viewing was a frustrating experience at best. The quality was usually poor and the playback could be very choppy - you'd often spend more time watching a "buffering" message on your screen than you would listening to the actual music or watching the video. Technology has come a long way since then, and today listening to streaming audio from your favorite Internet radio station on your computer or mobile device is a comparable experience to listening to a terrestrial (AM/FM) station on your radio.

In media theory, there is a concept of *encoding and decoding*, which is helpful in understanding streaming audio or video. In the theoretical paradigm, the sender of the media message packages (encodes) the message, sends it through his or her selected media channels, and when it reaches its target, it is unpackaged (decoded) by the receiver (reader, viewer, or listener) allowing him or her to understand the message. This is an apt, if perhaps oversimplified, analogy of the way streaming works. When the audio content to be broadcast by your station (music, talk, etc.) is created on the broadcaster's end, it is encoded into bits by your broadcasting software (more on broadcasting software in Chapter 4) and transmitted in *packets* to your streaming server host. This data is then distributed to all the listeners who use various kinds of *players* to decode the data, turning it back into music or talk programming.

It is, in fact, *possible* to host your radio station using your own Internet connection, but since most consumer-level ISPs only allow around 2mbps (megabits per second) up-bandwidth, that would only allow you around 15 listeners at any given time if you're broadcasting at 128kbps - a standard bitrate for stations streaming music. A business-level service plan with your ISP, usually costing around $200 per month, generally allows about 5x this bandwidth, or 10mbps up, which would still max you out at about 78 listeners. It just doesn't make sense to pay for all this bandwidth from your ISP, when you can use a streaming host provider for a fraction of the cost.

Choosing the streaming host that's right for you

A simple Google search of "Internet radio stream hosting" will return over a million results, so how do you begin to choose between all of these offerings? In order to pare down your choices, there are a number of factors you'll want to consider. They are:

- *Price*: Prices for stream hosting can vary wildly, and deciding whether something is "worth it" will depend on a number of different variables including your budget, the *bitrate* at which you're allowed to broadcast, the number of *listeners* allowed at that price, which *platforms* are provided, and the quality of *support* included in that price. You'll also need a host that is able to *scale* (increase your service level) as your station grows. All of these aspects are discussed below.

- *Bitrate*: When audio files are compressed, they have pieces of the file - usually frequencies not audible by the human ear - removed in order to make the file smaller. The bitrate in audio compression refers to the amount of data the file may user per second of audio. Therefore, an mp3 encoded at 128 kbps will allow 128 *kilobits of data* for every second of audio. Files encoded at lower bitrates (32 or 64 kbps) will therefore allow much less data per second of audio, and the result will be lower audio fidelity. In the case of stream hosting, when a provider says they allow up to 128kbps bitrate, this refers to the amount of data accepted by the streaming server, so if you're broadcasting an mp3 encoded at 128kbps through a streaming server with a 128kbps limit, your listeners will hear the audio at the same fidelity as the original file. If, however, your streaming server limits you to a 64kbps bitrate, your file will be encoded down by your broadcasting software to this level, resulting in the listener hearing the file at a much lower quality than the original. The important thing to remember is that the higher the bitrate, the higher quality audio your listeners will hear. As a rule of thumb, most music stations broadcast at either 128, 192, or 320kbps (usually the differences between these are barely perceptible) while all-talk stations can get away with broadcasting at 64 or even 32kbps.

- *Bandwidth*: Bandwidth refers to the amount of data that may be transferred to your listeners over a given period of time. One important thing to remember about bandwidth is that it will *only* get used up when listeners are connected to your station. Determining how much bandwidth you'll use requires some very simple math, and depends on the *bitrate* at which your broadcasting, your number of *listeners*, and the amount of *time* spent listening. Let's take a very simple example - let's say you have 10 listeners listening to an hour-long show, broadcast at 128kbps. Each listener is consuming 460,800 kilobits or 57.6 Megabytes over the course of the hour. Multiply this by 10 listeners, and collectively they have consumed 576 Megabytes, or just over a half a gigabyte of bandwidth. Some hosting providers provide unlimited bandwidth, some impose bandwidth limits, and still others provide pay-as-you-go plans, where you only pay for the amount of bandwidth used

- *Listeners*: Like bitrate and bandwidth, the number of simultaneous *listeners* allowed by a streaming host is another parameter that you'll want to consider when making your selection. This is one of the trickier considerations, as I'm sure you're very optimistic about the number of listeners you'll be getting for your station. It's important, though, to think realistically, and to understand that as your station gets off the ground, the number of listeners may be low, especially during those first few months. Many streaming host plans offer tiered packages with prices increasing as you go from 75 to 100 to 500 to 1000 or more listeners. Try to resist going for the "Platinum" plan right from the beginning, as you'll only be purchasing additional headroom for more listeners which you may or may not get. On the other hand, you don't want to get caught with a runaway hit show, and not have enough bandwidth to serve them, or your listener cap will cut some of your listeners off. It is precisely for this reason that scalability, discussed next, should be a key factor in your decision.

- *Scalability*: Simply put, scalability is the ability to increase your bandwidth and/or listener limits at a moment's notice without any interruption in your service. Taking the example cited above, if you find yourself broadcasting a show that turns out to be a runaway hit, or an event with a listener count that far exceeds your expectations, you'll want a provider that will be able to increase your limits without causing any downtime on your stream or interruption for your listeners. Look at each prospective host's plans carefully - you should be able to determine whether they allow this kind of scalability. Many hosts offer tiered plans that can be upgraded on the fly simply by logging in to their admin control panel and changing your plan yourself, instantly switching you from the lower to the higher tier. Still others offer "pay as you go" plans, where you only pay for the bandwidth used.

- *Platform*: There are 2 kinds of audio streaming servers that will be available from prospective streaming hosts - SHOUTcast and Icecast. The choice between the two can be confusing for the first time Internet radio producer, so I'll offer a brief rundown on the pros and cons of each.

SHOUTcast

Pros: As far as I can tell, the number one benefit from choosing a SHOUTcast server, and the reason I believe most people choose this option, is that your station gets listed in the SHOUTcast server directory, which is likewise syndicated to other radio directories, offering exposure to thousands of potential listeners.

Cons: SHOUTcast doesn't allow "mount points" which allow seamless switching between AutoDJ (part of the Centova control panel used by many streaming hosts) and a live stream. There is currently no way to switch between the two without an interruption in your broadcast.

Icecast

Pros: Icecast provides "mount points" which not only allow your broadcast to seamlessly switch between AutoDJ and a live stream, but also allow for multiple streams simultaneously, provided you stay within your allocated bitrate. For example, if you wanted to set up a live remote with a broadcaster streaming from the field, and you have a 320kbps bitrate limit, you could have 2 streams operating simultaneously at 128kbps, using a total of 256kbps, well within your 320kbps limit. Mount points also make it a much simpler matter to relay other streams to yours than it would be with SHOUTcast.

Cons: Your station is listed in the Icecast directory, which gives you exposure to fewer potential listeners than you would get with SHOUTcast.

At Radio Free Brooklyn, we opted to go with an Icecast server, mainly because of the mount point functionality. In terms of quality, both are about equal, it's just a matter of which platform's functionality best aligns with the goals for your station that you considered in the previous chapter.

Support: Although one hopes to never use it, there is nothing like a solid support system in place when you need it. I can't overstate the importance of quality support when it comes to choosing a stream hosting provider - or any vendor for that matter. Research each prospective provider's support system carefully. Do they provide around-the-clock support for those times when your stream may go down at 3 in the morning? What is their response time? Do they provide support via phone, online chat, or email? Unfortunately, bad things can and do happen, and you want to make sure you're protected in the event something goes wrong. If you've found a provider with good service at a good price, but they don't provide quality support, move on. It's worth spending a little more for the peace of mind of knowing that you'll be supported if things should start to go awry.

Community: Another thing to consider when choosing a provider is whether or not there is an active community of users for that particular service. Often, a provider will set up message boards or forums for its users, allowing them to talk to each other about the service, often answering each other's questions and giving each other tips. Such forums can be a fantastic resource when you have a question about a particular aspect of the service that you don't feel is critical enough to open a support ticket. Just perusing the boards can provide you with an education in audio streaming and Internet radio in general, and may save you from hours of fruitless Googling of a question you'd like to have answered. It's also not uncommon in such communities for another user to answer your question even more quickly than would a support technician. Before you choose a provider, spend a little time in their forums and try to get an idea of the level of satisfaction users have with the service, as well as any recurring problems or issues they might be having.

Control Panel: One of the things you want to be sure to check on is what kind of back-end control you'll have over your stream. It seems that most radio stream providers these days are using the Centova Control Panel (http://www.centova.com/en/cast) Among the many features of Centova are: web-based stream configuration; AutoDJ - a programmable automatic fallback to your live stream that can provide programming and playlist scheduling even when there's no DJ in the studio; the ability to monitor the number of listeners in real time; detailed listener statistics and royalty reports; the ability to monitor and stop/start/reload your stream from the web; and the ability to add or remove mount points and stream relays (for Icecast servers).

Case study: Radio Free Brooklyn

At Radio Free Brooklyn, we opted to go with an Icecast server - mainly because of the ability to add mount points, since we planned on doing a fair number of remote broadcasts. The provider we chose offered an Icecast plan that gave us the ability to broadcast at 128kbps with unlimited listeners and unmetered bandwidth, for $33.00 per month. This seemed like a good deal, so we signed up and immediately launched a "test feed" - essentially an "always on" stream of music that I set up to broadcast from my laptop computer. We tested the stream for six weeks, and didn't have any issues or complaints. It seemed like we had found our host.   The first sign that something was amiss came when I received a call from a friend who was listening, saying that the stream sounded "choppy." I listened from my phone and confirmed that, indeed, the stream was having some major problems - I would hear one second of audio, followed by one second of silence, over and over. I was able to log into the Centova Control Panel from my phone and restart the stream, but the problem persisted. I immediately put in a call to support and got a voice mail, so I emailed the support team informing them of the issue. I never got any response from their support team. The problem did eventually clear up, which makes me think that they *did* get my messages, but I still received no communication.

The second issue came on the day of our first live remote broadcast. We'd set up a mount point to broadcast from an event, and when the event started we switched off the broadcast from the studio (using Chrome Remote Desktop) and started the new stream. About ten minutes into the broadcast, the broadcasting software began throwing an error saying the stream couldn't be found. Upon checking my email, I saw I had been sent an automatic message informing me that our stream had shut down because we had "exceeded our bandwidth." I knew this wasn't possible because we were broadcasting at 128kbps, and our other source in the studio was turned off completely. We tried again, and again we were shut down, this time after only a few minutes. I got on the phone to support, and once again got their voice mail. I went to my computer and put in an emergency support ticket. I got no response for over 8 hours, long after the event was over. So much for support.

This story does have a happy ending, however. The good news is that these events led us to a streaming host that seems much better suited to our needs. Not only do they have a solid support system, but they also boast a robust user community, and offer a pay-as-you-go plan that saves us money by only charging us for the bandwidth we use. I won't reveal the name of the first hosting company, but you can find the new one at http://internet-radio.com.

As you can see, there's quite a lot to consider when choosing a streaming host, and since this decision is one of the most important ones you'll make, start your research early so you don't get caught, as we did, with your pants down!

Chapter 3

Getting Set Up – Building A Studio

Now that you've established some goals for your station, and hopefully started thinking about stream host providers, let's focus on your studio itself. You don't need to spend a lot of money on equipment, and many of the pieces of gear we'll discuss in this chapter can be found used on craigslist or eBay at a fraction of the original cost.

The Studio Space

Even if you don't have a designated room in which to put your studio, it's a good idea to at least have a designated area you can dedicate to broadcasting, especially if you'll be doing live shows. The most important consideration, of course, is how your broadcast will sound, so try to find a space that is as quiet as possible. You'll be surprised at how much ambient sound a good microphone can pick up, so try to choose an area that isn't too close to a window (especially if you live in the city) or interior ambient noises like air conditioners, fans, dishwashers, etc. Chances are that, unless you build out a fully equipped sound studio, you will pick up some ambient noise here and there, but you can minimize this by careful selection of your designated studio space. At Radio Free Brooklyn, our studio is in the basement of a bicycle shop, which is shielded from most outside and interior noise, but we still get the occasional whirr of a power tool, or the distinctive whooshing sound of an air hose filling a bicycle tire. Instead of seeing this as a liability, however, we've turned it into an asset. Broadcasting from the basement of a local business has become part of RFB's narrative, and gotten us lots of press. It's an element of our brand in that it emphasizes that we are a small, independent, community-focused organization. Now every time a broadcast is punctuated by the sounds of a bike shop doing business, it provides our hosts with an opportunity to emphasize to their listeners that we do, in fact, broadcast from the basement of a local bike shop. It's also proved to be a great business generator for the owners of the shop!

A further consideration when choosing a space is the design and construction of the area itself. Try to avoid rooms that have concrete floors and walls, as these will reflect sound and cause echoes that will bounce around the room and potentially affect the sound of your broadcast. If this type of room is your only option, try to lay down rugs or other materials that are sound absorbent and will dampen the sound and minimize echoes. Corners, in particular, can cause sound to reflect in ways that may be undesirable, so if your space has sharp corners you may try to mitigate echoing by filling them with foam or other materials that will absorb and not reflect vibrations. Furniture blankets (the ones used by movers) are particularly good at absorbing sound and are a much more inexpensive option than purchasing professional sound-absorbing panels.

Microphones

As mentioned earlier in this book, the minimum pieces of gear you'll need to start your station are a computer and a good microphone. The mic may be the most important hardware purchase you'll make, as it's the primary determinant of sound quality, so it's good to consider lots of options to ensure you make the right choice. Microphones can range in cost from the very inexpensive (under $50) to the prohibitively expensive (thousands of dollars), so what you want to look for is a good balance between quality and price. A lower price point doesn't *necessarily* mean lower quality, and many great mics can be found for a great price.

USB or Analog - Which should I choose?

One of the first decisions you'll face when shopping for a mic is whether to get a USB mic that plugs directly into your computer, or a traditional analog mic with a 3-pin XLR connector. The main benefit of a USB mic is that it will plug directly into your computer and eliminate the need for an audio interface or mixing board. This may be a good way to go if all you'll be doing is playing music from iTunes and voice broadcasting, but if you want to bring other elements into your broadcasts like CDs and vinyl, you may want to consider an analog mic that you can plug in to an audio interface or mixing board (more on mixing boards later in this chapter.)

Additionally, there are a few other downsides to USB mics that bear mentioning. USB mics are powered by internal preamps and analog-to-digital converters that can vary wildly in quality. Inexpensive USB microphones with sub-par preamps and convert-ers can have a negative effect on the quality of the audio coming through the mic. Further, if you want to have guests on your radio shows, they will need mics as well, and most computers have a limited number of USB ports. It is much simpler to have mics that you can plug into dedicated channels on a board, which will also give you greater control over individual mic levels during your broadcasts. Finally, because you'll always want to monitor your broadcasts using headphones, having multiple USB microphones attached to your computer might cause problems. There will likely be a latency, or delay, between speech going into a USB mic and what you hear in the headphones on your computer. Some USB mics afford the opportunity to monitor the sound directly from the mic, but if you have more than one mic going into your computer you may find yourself unable to monitor them all.

If you do decide to go with a USB mic, a couple that we've heard good reports on are the **Rode Podcaster USB Dynamic Mic** (around $200 new), and the **Blue Yeti USB Condenser Mic** (around $130 new.)

If you're using a mixing board or an audio interface, an analog mic will be the way to go. Again, there are many tried-and-true mics out there, several of which can be purchased without breaking the bank. The most important quality you'll want to look for in any mic is the sound - you want something that delivers a warm, human sound without picking up too much ambient noise. Of course, how a mic sounds can often depend on both the voice that it's picking up, as well as individual tastes and opinions on what sounds "good." Go to your local music shop and ask a sales person if you can test out some of the mics they have for sale. Spend some time listening to how your voice is represented through each one, and then choose the one that sounds best to you. The Transom website (a great website for both broadcasters and podcasters) has a fantastic resource called the "Studio Mic Shootout" (http://tran-som.org/2005/transom-studio-mic-shootout/) where you can listen to recordings from several mics "blindly," meaning that you don't immediately see which mic you're listening to. When you've found one with a sound you like, you can then reveal the "Mic Shootout Key" to see which microphone you've chosen. It's a great way to select a quality mic without being swayed by brand name or price. A good way to use this tool is to make a note of your top 4 or 5 microphones, so if your first selection is out of your price range, you'll have other options.

Another major consideration when shopping for an analog mic is whether to get a *dynamic* or *condenser* microphone. Dynamic mics are excellent voice mics, and can go a long way towards eliminating unwanted ambient noise from your broadcast. One downside to dynamic mics, however, is that they tend to have low output, and require quality gain from your mixing board or interface. They also tend to pick up radio and/or electrical interference more readily than condenser mics, so this is something to watch out for as well. Condenser mics don't need as much help from external preamps, but they are more sensitive, and tend to pick up more room noise and ambient sound than dynamic mics. Once again, the determining factor when choosing a microphone should be how the mic sounds to you. Both condenser and dynamic mics can be excellent studio mics. Keep in mind that condenser mics often require *phantom power* - which is an additional 48v of power supplied by your board or interface to power the mic. If you're using condensers, make sure that your whatever you're plugging them into has phantom power capabilities.

At Radio Free Brooklyn, we use a **Rode NT-1** large diaphragm condenser mic (around $200 new) for the host mic, which delivers a nice, bright, focused sound. For our guest mics, we use a pair of **Audio Technica AT2020** large diaphragm condenser mics that, at around $100 new, is one of the better values out there when it comes to inexpensive quality mics. Both of these mics use what's called a *cardioid* pattern, meaning that they will pick up what's in front of it, but very little sound from the sides or back, allowing for better sound isolation.

Other analog microphone that we've heard good reports from include the **Electovoice EV RE-20** (around $400-$500 new) which is a bit more expensive than some of the other mics mentioned here, but has become standard in many professional radio stations due to it's warm sound and tight pickup pattern that eliminates unwanted room noise. **The Rode Procaster** (the analog version of the Rode Podcaster mentioned above) may be a more affordable alternative, with a price point of around $200-$250 new. This mic has also received excellent reviews for its sound, and boasts many of the same attributes as the more expensive alternatives.

Audio Interfaces and Mixing Boards

If you've decided to go analog with your microphone, you'll need a way to get the audio signal into your computer. There are two ways to go here: audio interface or mixing board. Since audio interfaces generally have a very limited number of inputs (usually 2-4), and usually don't provide much granular control over things like EQ, they can be great for getting vocal mics into your computer but won't be of much use when it comes to other devices that you may want to add to your mix. For that reason, this section will focus mainly on mixing boards - but if you do want to purchase an audio interface (they can be great to bring with you to live remote broadcasts) some of the better brands to look for include M-Audio, Focusrite, Mackie, and Tascam.

Mixing boards, on the other hand, offer much greater flexibility when it comes to adding external devices to your broadcast, and can range in size from very tiny - like the **Alesis MultiMix 4 USB FX 4-Channel Mixer** (around $80 new) - to the much larger and feature-rich **BEHRINGER XENYX X2442USB** (around $350 new). One of the key things to look for when shopping for a mixing board is the ability to connect to your computer using USB. This will allow you to send your main mix back into your computer where it can be picked up by your broadcasting software (covered in Chapter 4) and sent to your streaming server. The number of channels you'll need in your board will be determined by the number of *peripherals* (CD players, turntables, etc.) you'll want to plug in and have available for your broadcasts. At Radio Free Brooklyn, we use a **BEHRINGER XENYX X2222USB** (around $250 new), a 16-channel board that produces a nice, warm sound and features 8 microphone inputs with studio-grade compression available on each mic channel, 3-band EQ, and an FX processor with 16 presets. Depending on your setup, you may not need 16 channels, but to give you an idea of how we utilize the board, I've included a rundown of what we have plugged into our mixing board (this is illustrated in figure 3-2 at the end of this chapter):

- Channel 1 - Host Microphone

- Channel 2 - Guest Mic 1

- Channel 3 - Guest Mic 2

- Channel 4 - Open Channel (for extra mics or peripherals we may need to add)

- Channels 5 & 6 - Turntables channeled through a turntable mixer (Channel 5 for left channel, Channel 6 for right channel)

- Channels 7 & 8 - Dual CD Player/Mixer (Channel 7 for left channel, Channel 8 for right channel)

- Channel 9/10 - Laptop (or other audio devices such as tablets, iPhones, iPods, etc.)

- Channel 11/12 - Alesis i/o dock which houses an iPad 2

- Channel 13/14 - Open Channel

- Channel 15/16 - Studio computer which plays music through MegaSeg (more on MegaSeg in Chapters 4 & 5)

Clearly, if you don't have as many peripherals, you may not need as large a board, and you'll find many, many options for mixing boards in all sizes and configurations. As with mics, your individual needs will dictate your final choice, but two brands that we highly recommend are Behringer and Mackie - it's hard to go wrong with either of these.

Peripherals

I'm not going to go into too much detail when it comes to peripherals, since there is obviously a huge range of options available to you, and your choices of peripherals will vary significantly depending on your budget and the needs of your radio station. However, to give you an idea of the kinds of peripherals available, and to demonstrate that most can be purchased at very reasonable prices, I will provide a very quick rundown of what we have available to our hosts at Radio Free Brooklyn - along with their associated costs.

- *Turntables* - Many DJs today no longer spin actual vinyl, although **Serato Scratch** is hugely popular and utilizes turntables with "control vinyl" to emulate the traditional DJ experience. For many years, the **Technics 1200** was the industry standard for DJs, but these turntables can be prohibitively expensive, especially since they are no longer manufactured and demand is unusually high. Instead, we use two **Audio Technica AT-LP120** turntables (about $250 each), which are essentially clones of the 1200 and get the job done just as effectively. Purists may argue with me on the latter point, but for our purposes, they work well. The turntables are plugged into a **Stanton M203 2-Channel DJ Mixer** (around $100 new), providing granular control over the turntable mix and crossfades, which is plugged into channels 5 & 6 on our mixing board.

- *Dual CD Player* - CDs are sadly going the way of the dinosaur, but some of our hosts and DJs still use them. To accommodate, we provide a **Gemini CDM4000 Dual CD**

Player with Mixer (around $200 new.) This functions in much the same way as the turntables and mixer except that it has everything - 2 CD players and a mixer - contained in a single unit. The CD player has balanced XLR outputs, and is plugged into channels 7 & 8 on our mixing board.

- *Alesis i/o Dock for iPad* - The **i/o Dock from Alesis** (around $200 new) is a fantastic little device that allows your iPad to become a pro-audio tool by providing audio inputs and outputs. We have the dock mounted on a laptop stand with the outputs plugged into channel 11/12 on the mixing board. Now, anything that is played on the iPad can be channeled through the board, and by channeling the control room mix from the board to the inputs, we've created a two-way device that can take phone calls to the studio using Skype (more on this later.) Another primary use of the iPad and dock is DJing using the excellent **Djay 2** app from Algoriddim. Djay 2 not only allows you to create mixes from your own music library, but it's one of the only DJ apps that will work with Spotify, essentially giving you access to a library of over 20 million songs. When the iPad is not employed as a DJ app or taking phone calls, it serves as the studio's official time clock (using the 'Clocks' app) allowing our hosts to time the beginnings and endings of their shows to the second. Since all our automation (described in Chapter 6) is based on our studio computer's internal clock, governed by a network clock, the iPad - which is tuned to the same network clock - is never out of sync with our automation systems.

- *Laptop* - We don't actually have a studio laptop, but have set up a station that includes a laptop stand and a 35mm connector plugged into channel 9/10 on our board. This way, our hosts can use their laptops to play music through iTunes, Ableton Live, Spotify, or any one of the vast array of audio software options available. Since the connector is just a 35mm plug converted to a balanced TRS connector cable being fed into the board, this allows other devices with a 35mm connection - like tablets and iPhones - to be connected here as well.

- *Studio Computer* - Our studio computer, a 27-inch iMac, is the heart of our operation and will be discussed in greater detail in subsequent chapters. For now, suffice it to say that the studio computer is the one that plays all the non-live, scheduled programming from **MegaSeg**, can be used by our hosts to play music, and also contains the broadcasting software that sends our signal to the streaming host. This is plugged into the "always on" channel 15/16 on our board.

Studio Monitors/Speakers

Hosts performing live broadcasts are unlikely to want to spend their entire show tethered to their headphones to monitor their show. For this reason, it's a good idea to connect a pair of studio monitors to the mixing board so that the hosts can listen to their show in the studio whenever they're not on the microphone. Using one of the pairs of lines out for the main mix, you can connect a pair of studio monitors to the mixing board using either TRS (balanced) 1/4" cable, or balanced XLR cable, depending on the capabilities of your board. We use a pair of **M-Audio Studiophile AV 40 Active Studio Monitor Speakers** (about $100 per pair new) which are inexpensive powered monitors that deliver a *flat frequency response* - meaning that the speakers aren't designed to do things like give an additional boost to the bass or other frequencies, allowing you to hear exactly what is being output to your listeners.

Positioning the speakers in the studio will depend on a combination of personal preference and the way your room is set up. At RFB we have the monitors mounted on the wall opposite the host, angled at roughly 45 degrees so that the host would be at the apex of the triangle [see figure 3-1].

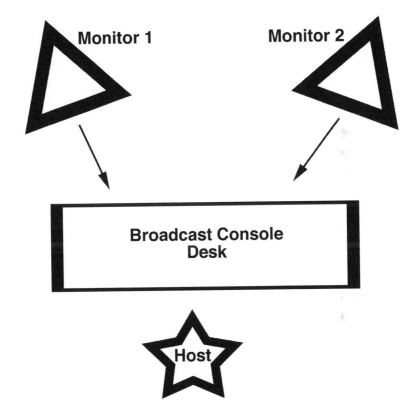

Figure: 3-1

Once you've got the speakers connected, you'll need a way for the host to adjust the volume or mute the speakers completely. If the volume on the speakers is up while the host is on the microphone, the sound from the speakers will be picked up by the mic, causing potentially equipment-damaging (or worse, ear-damaging) feedback. To avoid this, you can get a little volume attenuator called the **SM Pro Nano Patch** (about $60 new), which can be inserted in your signal chain between the mixing board and the speakers so that the volume can be adjusted without having to adjust it on the speakers themselves.

How to take call-ins using the mixing board and an iPad in your studio

If you mixing board has multiple output jacks for the main mix, such as TRS outputs in addition to XLR, or a pair of *control room outputs*, then it's very easy to set up a system to take calls on your live broadcasts. They way we have it set up at RFB is that the Alesis i/o dock housing an iPad outputs its signal to the iPad channel on the mixing board, and the dock's inputs are fed from the control room outputs on the board. We then use Skype on the iPad (which has its own phone number - see Skype's help pages for how to set up your own number.) The caller hears the mix from the board, and the host and audience hears the caller who is now part of the main mix, as their voice is being fed into the iPad channel.

Setting it all up

While this all may seem confusing as a list of connections, hopefully figure 3-2 will give you a better idea of how everything fits together. I hope that this chapter has given you at least a basic understanding of how to set up your Internet radio studio. You will, no doubt, want to make some adjustments for your particular situation, but the setup described here has worked well for Radio Free Brooklyn, and didn't cost us an arm and a leg!

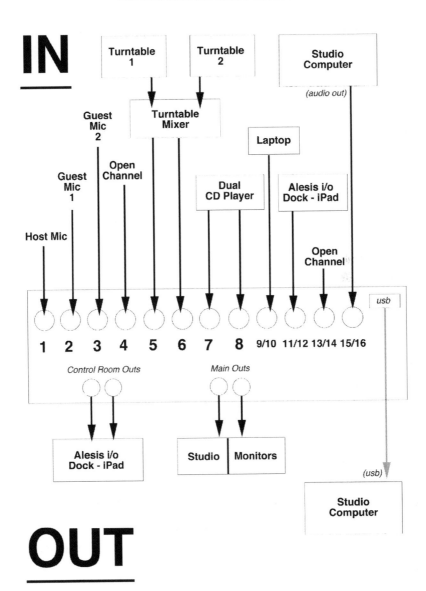

Figure: 3-2

Chapter 4

Unleashing Your Signal – Broadcasting Software

So you've purchased some equipment and your studio set up is underway - now what? Well, the most well-equipped studio in the world won't amount to a hill of beans in the world of Internet radio unless you can get that great sound from your studio to your streaming host, who will distribute it to your adoring listeners. To accomplish this, you'll have to obtain *broadcast software* that will encode your signal into the correct format and bitrate, and then send it off to your streaming host. No matter which platform you work with (Mac, PC, or Linux), you'll have options for broadcasting software that range from free to very expensive. In this chapter, we'll examine some of these options in the free or low-to-moderate price range, but you may want to do some additional research on your own as well. The full range of available software options can be overwhelming, and is beyond the scope of this book. What you'll find below are some of the most popular choices that will do the job without costing a lot of money. In addition to the options listed, it bears mentioning that some DJ Software now has the ability to broadcast your mix directly to your streaming host, but this isn't necessarily the best option if you're launching a 24/7 "always on" radio station. For a software tool that can handle a diverse array of programming, the four options listed below should provide you with a good starting point.

butt

Cost: Free
Platform: Windows, Mac OSX, Linux
Manufacturer: Open Source software
Download Website: http://butt.sourceforge.net/

Butt (which stands for Broadcast Using This Tool) is a free, open-source broadcasting solution that is very easy to set up and use. Using butt, you can broadcast to either SHOUTcast or Icecast servers, encoded into mp3 or ogg formats. Butt works on virtually any platform, and what the software may lack in aesthetic beauty, it more than makes up for in functionality. Some of the more prominent functions include the ability to record your broadcast, automatic connections to your streaming server on startup, the ability to send song metadata, like title and artist, to your server, and automatic reconnection if the connection has been interrupted. If you're on a tight budget, this free but robust software solution may be for you.

Nicecast

Cost: $59
Platform: Mac OSX
Manufacturer: Rogue Amoeba
Download Website: https://www.rogueamoeba.com/nicecast/

I happen to be a huge fan of Rogue Amoeba, manufacturer of a suite of excellent audio tools for the Mac OSX platform. While Nicecast, their broadcasting tool, exists exclusively for the Mac, it may be even easier than butt to set up and use, and is certainly nicer to look at! Nicecast can broadcast to either SHOUTcast or Icecast streaming hosts, and boasts a *very* robust feature set including the ability to source your broadcast from virtually any audio device (such as your USB mixing board) or application (like iTunes or MegaSeg.) It even has a nifty little feature called the "application mixer" which allows you to split your source between an application and an audio device, giving you the ability to provide voiceover from your board while playing music from iTunes. Like Butt, Nicecast allows you to record your broadcast with the click of a single button and can also send song information to your server from virtually any source or application. The Rogue Amoeba team provides each user with individualized support and usually responds to inquiries within 24 hours. With a very attractive price point of just $59, Nicecast comes highly recommended, and is the solution we use at Radio Free Brooklyn.

SAM Broadcaster
Cost: $299
Platform: Windows
Manufacturer: Spacial
Download Website: http://spacial.com/sam-broad-caster

While it will cost you some money up front, SAM Broadcaster is a very popular choice for those working exclusively with Windows PCs. SAM is an extremely feature-rich software, and includes such bells and whistles as: a professional audio processor with EQ, stereo expander and multi-band processor; real-time listener statistics; a "smart" crossfader that automatically detects the best point in a song to start fading tracks; automation tools to keep your station running when you're out of the studio; web widgets so you can incorporate "now playing" info into your website, and the ability to stream in multiple formats (mp3, ogg, AAC, and wma.) For those who want to give SAM Broadcaster a whirl without plunking down 300 dollars up front, they do have a monthly subscription option that allows you to use a cloud-based version of SAM for a subscription price of $15 per month. Once again, SAM Broadcaster is currently Windows-only, but Mac users, don't despair - there is apparently a Mac version in the works that will hopefully be released very soon.

RadioDJ

Cost: Free
Platform: Windows
Download Website: http://www.radiodj.ro/

RadioDJ is one of the newer entrants into the world of broadcasting software, and seems to be a very promising contender, but it is, like SAM Broadcaster, a solution that will only work for Windows users. Some of RadioDJ's features are: support for both SHOUTcast and Icecast streams; the ability to stream in a variety of formats (mp3, wav, wma, flac, and ac3); Auto DJ mode for 24/7 automation; the ability to add audio processing (via plugin) with automatic gain control, compressor, and 10-band EQ. Although RadioDJ is free and appears to have an active community of users, both major plusses, I will offer one caveat which is that it may require a bit more technical expertise to get up and running than some of the other "out of the box" solutions. You will have to set up your own MySQL database on your computer in order for the software to function. For those that are comfortable with this, the feature-set offered by this free software package make giving a try a worthwhile endeavor.

Chapter 5

Putting It All Together – DIY Automation

For those readers who are interested in running a fully automated 24/7 streaming radio station, your automation protocols will be at the heart of your operation. They can also be the most challenging aspect of your station to get up and running, so in this chapter we'll focus on how to use available software to create an automation system that allows you to both perform live broadcasts as well as broadcast scheduled pre-recorded shows (including re-broadcasts of live shows.) Once again, please bear in mind that the solutions offered in this chapter are heavily geared towards Mac users and that a Windows user may find that their options include much simpler ways of doing things; but the Windows user may also find some value in examining the logic behind the solutions described here, using it to create his or her own customized solution. I would also like to point out that the Prometheus Radio Project (http://www.prometheusradio.org) - an advocacy group dedicated to assisting independent broadcasters - has an excellent guide to radio automation that provides a detailed rundown on options available to users of Mac, PC, Linux and BeOS, along with case studies for each solution. However, even with this outstanding guide I found that, as a Mac user, I wasn't able to use these off-the-shelf solutions to do exactly what I needed for Radio Free Brooklyn, and so had to create my own custom protocols, which are described in this chapter.

Automation Software

In the previous chapter, I described two broadcasting software solutions that advertise station automation as part of their feature set, so if you're a Windows user you may want to give one of these a try. If you're on a Mac, however, you'll most likely want to choose one of the software products below, customizing it using the processes described later in the chapter.

> *Option 1 - MegaSeg Pro*
> Cost: $199
> Platform: Mac OSX
> Manufacturer: Fidelity Media
> Download Website: http://www.megaseg.com

MegaSeg is easily one of the most popular choices for radio automation among broadcasters who rely on Macs to run their station. One of the nice things about MegaSeg is that, in addition to its invaluable automation features, MegaSeg can also function as DJ software, giving your hosts granular control over beat matching, mixing, and sound effects. However, it's the automation features that provide the real value to MegaSeg although it's fair to warn the newbie that there may be a moderate learning curve before you are completely comfortable using it. MegaSeg integrates well with iTunes and also works with a variety of DJ controllers such as the **Pioneer DDJ-WeGO, DDJ-S1, DDJ-SX** or **NuMark's NS6, DJ2GO**, and the **Hercules RMX**. Due to its relatively low price-point, ease of use, excellent customer support, and programmable automation features, MegaSeg is currently the automation solution of choice in our studio at Radio Free Brooklyn, and will be the software used in the custom solutions provided in the case studies later in this chapter.

Option 2 - Radiologik DJ Station and Scheduler
Cost: $249
Platform: Mac OSX
Manufacturer: MacinMind Software
Download Website: http://www.macinmind.com/Radiologik

For Mac users, Radiologik by MacinMind is easily the number 1 competitor to MegaSeg, providing a number of similar automation features, but a logic and interface that is wildly different. Whereas MegaSeg integrates with iTunes by importing playlists into its own database, Radiologik actually uses iTunes as the database itself, using iTunes Smart Playlist feature to select songs, and integrating with its own "top logic" which utilizes a weekly scheduling system. Radiologik also boats a very active user community, an important feature that MegaSeg does *not* have, and that may be an important consideration when deciding which option is right for you. As I mentioned in the earlier chapter about finding a streaming host, user communities can be a great way to get support from others, often more quickly than you'd get from a company's support system, and also is a great resource for tricks and tips and for getting a reading on how fanatic (or frustrated) other users are before you make a commitment to buy.

Both MegaSeg and Radiologik offer free trial versions so you can download and play with both of them before you make your final decision. Although the trial versions are fully functional, each will "interrupt" you at 30-minute intervals, to remind you that you're using a trial version and ask if you're ready to buy. The free trials are still a good way to get a feel for the software before purchasing.

The rest of this chapter will be dedicated to providing the reader with specific use cases that I was confronted with when building an integrated automation system for Radio Free Brooklyn. Although your goals may differ from ours, it is my hope that you will find something in these case studies that will be useful to you when building out a system of your own.

Case study: Automation Protocols for Trafficking Pre-Programmed Shows for Broadcast

The Problem:

One of the toughest issues I encountered when building our automation protocols was how to create system that would allow hosts of pre-programmed shows to upload or submit their finished audio files, and have them trafficked at the right time to the right folders to be picked up by MegaSeg for broadcast - all without intervention by a human being. Given that we launched our station with 35 shows, it just wasn't practical to traffic everything by hand, as that would quickly consume many more waking hours than I was willing to provide. Additionally, I wanted to give the hosts ample time during the week - with a deadline of just a few hours before their show - to get their files submitted. A secondary goal was to provide a way for these hosts to queue, or "bank," several episodes at once so that if they recorded multiple episodes at a time, they could be broadcast each week in the correct order. None of these were things that MegaSeg could provide on its own, but with a little resourcefulness, I cobbled together a system that works quite well.

> *The Tools:*
> MegaSeg
> Dropbox (http://www.dropbox.com)
> Hazel (http://www.noodlesoft.com/hazel.php)

The Solution:

I'm assuming, for brevity's sake, that Dropbox needs no introduction to the savvy Internet user these days. As the go-to solution for sharing files across networks, it seemed like a natural choice for having hosts submit their radio shows for broadcast. But how, then, would MegaSeg know which files to pick up from which folders, or when to broadcast them, for that matter? This is where Hazel comes in. Hazel is a brilliant automation plugin created by Noodlesoft Software for Mac users that is very similar to Mac's own "Automator" application. Hazel, however, has more robust functionality, making it an extremely useful tool for building out automation processes. From Hazel's website:

> *Hazel watches whatever folders you tell it to, auto-matically organizing your files according to the rules you create. It features a rule interface similar to that of Apple Mail so you should feel right at home. Have Hazel move files around based on name, date, type, what site/email address it came from (Safari and Mail only) and much more. Automatically put your music in your Music folder, movies in Movies. Keep your downloads off the desktop and put them where they are supposed to be*

This is exactly what Hazel does, and does it beautifully. Here, step-by-step, is how we integrated Hazel with Dropbox to create a solution to our trafficking challenge. We'll use a single user (we'll call him Bill) in our example, and we'll say that Bill is the host of a (fictional) show called *Brooklyn Happy Hour* that airs every Wednesday at 8pm. The process outlined here, however, will be the same for all hosts of pre-programmed shows, with times and folder names adjusted appropriately.

1. A Dropbox folder is created within our Radio Free Brooklyn Dropbox folder, named "Brooklyn Happy Hour" with the path Dropbox/Radio Free Brooklyn/Shows/Brooklyn Happy Hour - and this folder is shared with Bill. Bill only has access to this show folder and the sub-folders contained within it.

2. Within "Brooklyn Happy Hour," three subfolders are created, called BHH-LATEST, BHH-QUEUE, BHH-ARCHIVE, and HOST FILES (BHH is code for the show name – *Brooklyn Happy Hour*.) Each folder serves a different function, as detailed below.

    a. BHH-LATEST - This is where Bill places his latest file if he is adding new files weekly (as opposed to queuing several up at a time.) Bill has until 5pm on Wednesday (3 hours before his show airs) to add his file to the BHH-LATEST folder, for reasons that will be apparent in the next step.

    b. BHH-QUEUE - If Bill wants to record several shows at once, or more frequently than once a week, he can instead add them to this folder, where they will be trafficked in the order in which they were created

    c. BHH-ARCHIVE - This folder will contain copies of the

last 5 shows that have already been trafficked.

d. HOST FILES - This folder has no automation associ-
    ated with it, but is simply a place for Bill to keep files
    related to his show that he may need to access from
    other computers.

3. Next, a Hazel "Rule," or set of rules, is applied to each of
    the subfolders.

    a. Folder: "BHH-LATEST"

    HAZEL RULES -

    At 5pm on Wednesday (3 hours before air time,)
    rename any file with the extension .mp3 to 'bhh_
    latest.mp3' and move to the broadcast queue folder
    - this is a separate folder that exists with the path
    "Dropbox/Radio Free Brooklyn/scheduled audio/
    Brooklyn Happy Hour/latest." This folder can actu-
    ally exist anywhere on your system, and doesn't nec-
    essarily need to live within the Dropbox hierarchy,
    but it should exist *outside* your host's show folder to
    prevent the host from inadvertently removing it or
    changing the file name. Make sure to select "replace
    the existing file" in the options for this action, so that
    it will overwrite whatever older file is currently in the
    broadcast queue.

Once the file has been renamed and moved to the broadcast queue
folder, the file is then *copied* back to BHH-ARCHIVE, and once
again renamed with the date added to the folder (which will be
the day of the show). After the file has been copied, renaming will
only affect the file copied to BHH-ARCHIVE, and won't affect the

name of 'bhh_latest' in the broadcast queue.

The way these rules would be expressed within Hazel are shown in figure 5.1:

Figure: 5-1

    b.   Folder: "BHH-QUEUE"

HAZEL RULES

First rule: At 4:45 on Wednesday (15 mins. before the previous rules run), identify the file that was *created first*, determined by they creation dates of the files in the folder. This allows you to identify which file should play next; assuming that the host created the shows in the order they were meant to air. Change the color label of this file to green (or the color of your choosing.)

Second rule: At 4:55 on Wednesday, identify the file with the green color label (this will be the file affected by the previous rule) and move it to the BHH-LAT-

EST folder. At this point, the BHH-LATEST rules described earlier will take over at 5pm and move the file to the broadcast queue.

The reason that this process utilizes two rules, spaced 10 minutes apart is that otherwise the rules would continue running after the correct file has been moved, and continue acting upon all the remaining files, moving each one to the BHH-LATEST folder until it's no longer 4:45pm. For this reason it's important to change one file and stop the process for a few minutes, so that a new process can begin and complete the move without affecting every file in the folder. These two rules, as expressed in Hazel, will look like this (figures 5-2 and 5-3):

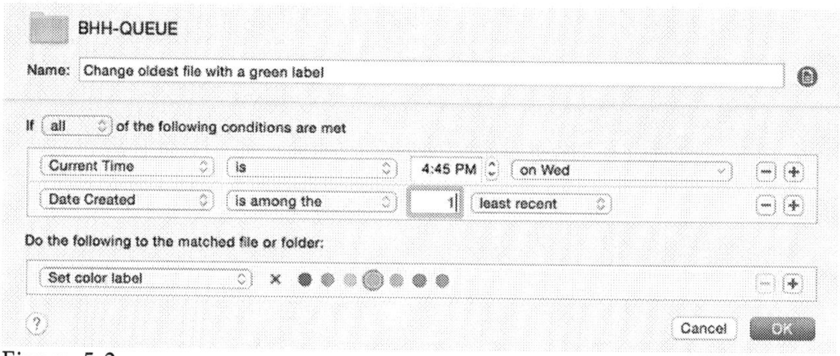

Figure: 5-2

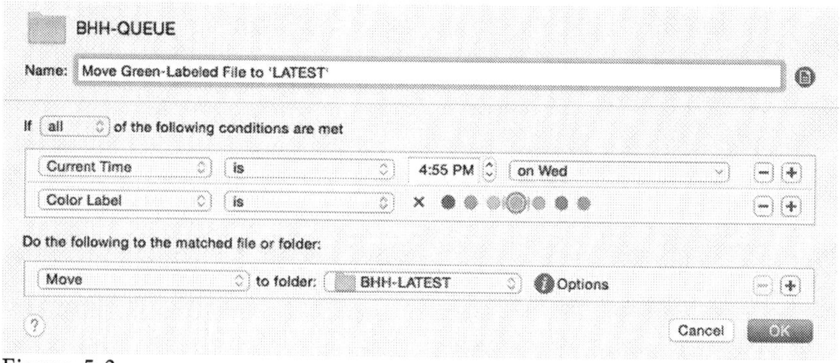

Figure: 5-3

NOTE: While the rules applied to the BHH-LATEST and BHH-QUEUE folders work perfectly on their own, it's best to use one or the other and not both. This is because if there's already something in the BHH-LATEST folder when the BHH-QUEUE rules run, it will be overwritten by whatever is moved from the queue folder. Advise your hosts to use one folder or the other, but never both at the same time.

c. Folder: "BHH-ARCHIVE"

HAZEL RULES

Since files added to the archive folder are placed there by other rules, this folder doesn't have any associated rules that affect the trafficking of show files. However, since audio files can be quite large, and an archive will build over time, it's important to keep the folder sizes manageable so as not to eat into your station computer's disk space. To accomplish this, we have created a rule that removes any file that is not among the five most recent, leaving only the 5 latest shows in the archive at any given time. In Hazel, this would be expressed in the simple rule illustrated in figure 5-4.

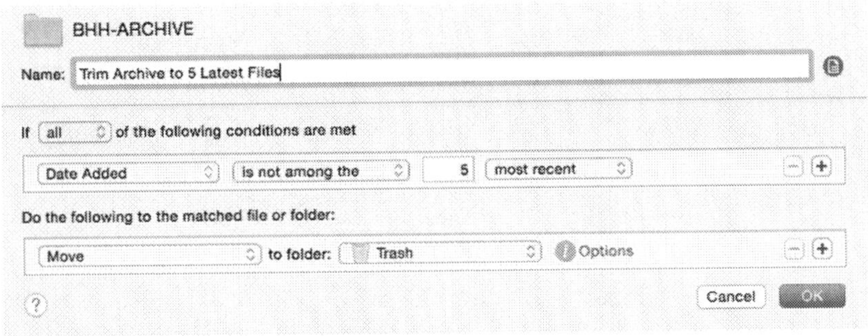

Figure: 5-4

    d. Folder: "HOST FILES"

HAZEL RULES -

Once again, this folder is for the host's personal use, so rules will have no effect on the broadcast. However, like the BHH-ARCHIVE folder, you may wish to apply your own rules to keep the hosts from loading up this folder with files that may eat into your station computer's disk space.

4. Set up MegaSeg to look for 'bhh_latest.mp3' in the same place every time "Brooklyn Happy Hour" is scheduled to air. In MegaSeg, the key features when it comes to scheduling regular shows are categories, playlists, and events, so we'll need to set up one of each in order for "Brooklyn Happy Hour" to play correctly. This can be done by executing the following steps.

    a. In MegSeg, create a category that will contain "Brooklyn Happy Hour" and only that show. In this case, let's call the category "PRE - Brooklyn Happy Hour." The reason I use the "PRE" prefix is so that when I'm looking at all the categories for all my shows arranged alphabetically, all of the pre-recorded shows are grouped together using the prefix "PRE." Similarly, I use the prefix "LRB" (for live re-broadcast) for live shows that are scheduled to re-air throughout the week, and "SYN" for all syndicated shows (more on syndicated shows later in this chapter.)

    b. Using the "Events" tab in MegaSeg's settings, create a one-time event that will import the show file ("bhh_latest") from the broadcast folder into the category

"PRE-Brooklyn Happy Hour" before their first show airs (see figure 5-5.1). We'll set this at 2 hours before the show's first airtime (figure 5-5.2), since by then the Hazel operations described earlier will all be complete. This step only needs to be done once, since the file name won't change, even when the file itself is swapped out for a new one the following week.

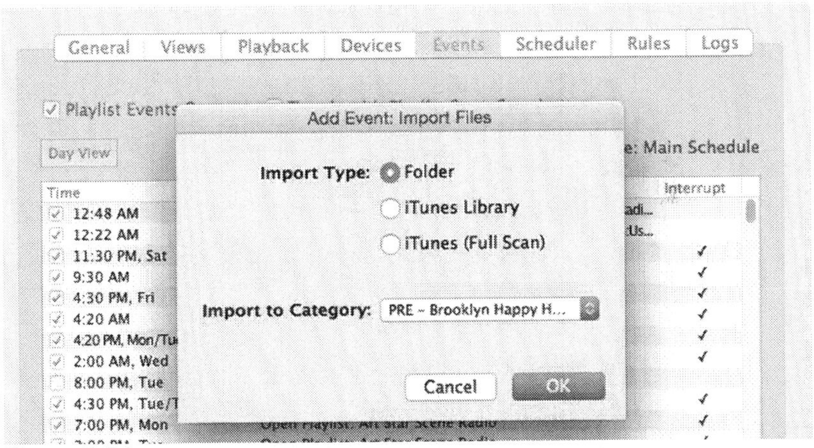

Figure: 5-5.1

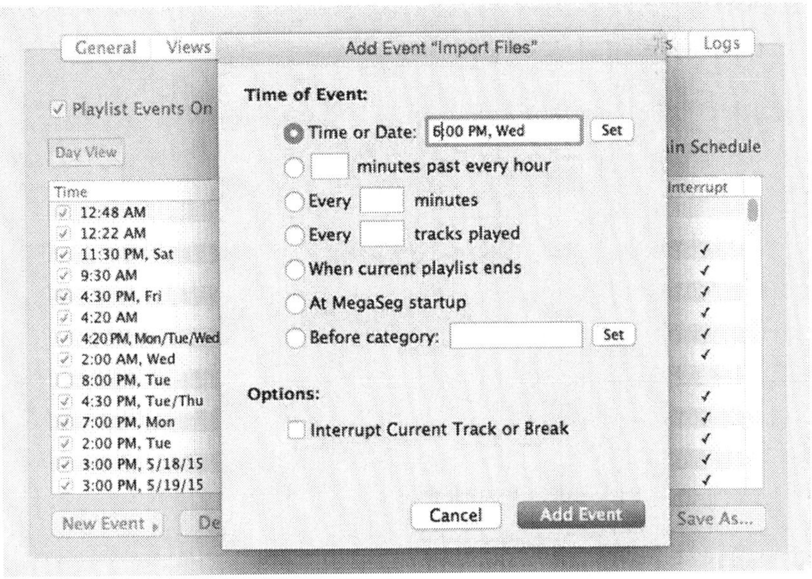

Figure: 5-5.2

c. Using the "Scheduler" tab in MegaSeg's settings, create a playlist that includes the category "PRE - Brooklyn Happy Hour." At RFB, each show's playlist begins with a file pulled from a category for station IDs so that an RFB station ID is heard before each show. This is followed by the show's category (in this case "PRE - Brooklyn Happy Hour"), which plays the show itself, since the show file ("bhh_latest") will be the only file in this category. If you wish, you can follow the show category with categories for more station IDs or filler content, just in case the show runs shorter than it's allocated time (figure 5-6.1). This will prevent dead air between the end of the show and the beginning of the next scheduled show. Save your playlist as "Brooklyn Happy Hour" (figure 5-6.2).

Figure: 5-6.1

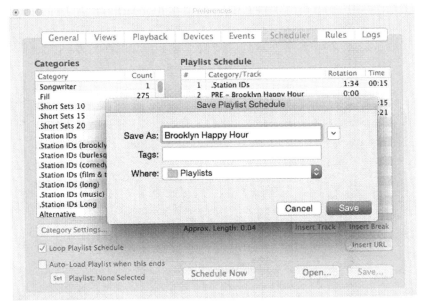

Figure: 5-6.2

d. Returning to the Events tab in Settings, you'll now create a *recurring* event that will load and play the "Brooklyn Happy Hour" playlist each time the show is scheduled to air. To do this, click "New Event => Open Playlist or Schedule" (figure 5-7.1) and select "Brooklyn Happy Hour" as the playlist to open (figure 5-7.2). Then, using the event scheduling features, make this a recurring event that will occur whenever the show is scheduled to air, in this case it will be every Wednesday at 8pm (figure 5-7.3). I also recommend ticking the "Interrupt Current Playlist or Schedule" box in the events scheduling interface, as this will ensure that your program will start exactly on time (figure 5-7.4)

Figure: 5-7.1

Figure: 5-7.2

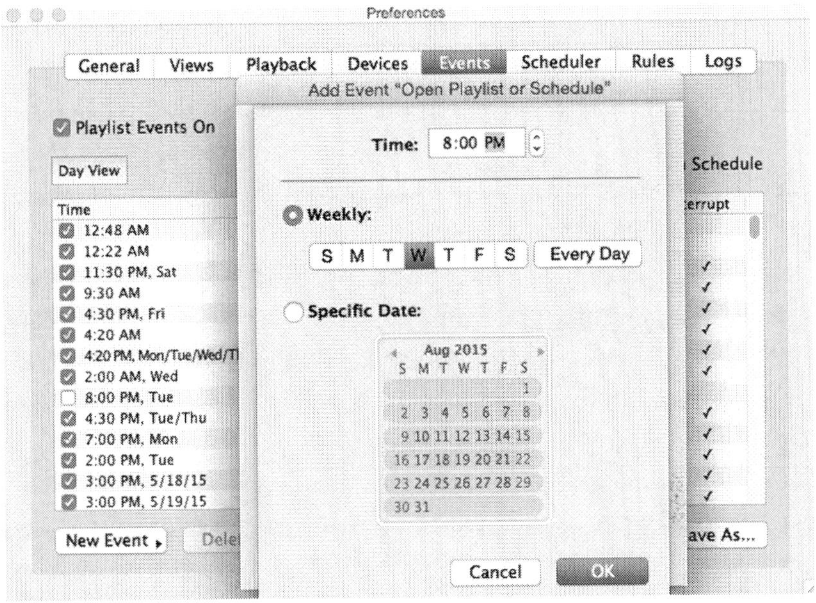

Figure: 5-7.3

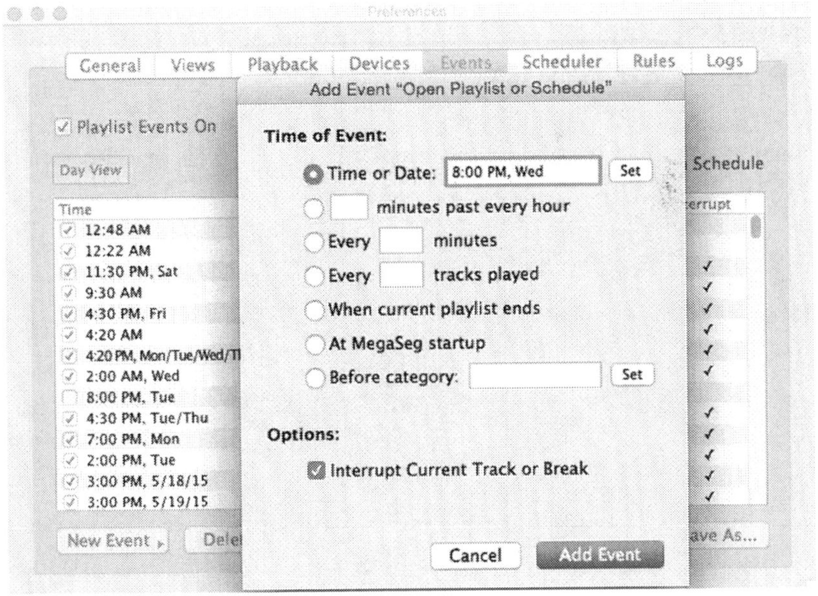

Figure: 5-7.4

So there you have it. We've just created our first automation protocol which, if executed correctly, will allow your hosts to add new
shows, queue them up for broadcast, and play them at the correct

time, without you having to lift a finger. Some of the steps may seem overly complicated at first glance, but the process is actually quite simple once you're familiar with it. It bears mentioning that the reason that I specify a three-hour advance time frame for moving files into the broadcast queue is less about the time the processes take to execute, and more about getting our hosts into the habit of getting their show files into their Dropbox folders well in advance. You may even want to give your hosts a 3-hour-before-air deadline, but not start the automation process until 2 hours before the show. That way, even if they are a little late (and trust me, some of them will be) they'll still have an hour grace period.

So now that we've seen how to effectively get pre-recorded shows into the broadcast queue, you may be asking yourself, "What about live shows? Is there a way to have a host perform live shows, record them, and automatically put the recordings into the broadcast queue for re-broadcasts?" I'm glad you asked! That process will be covered in the next case study.

Case study: Protocols for Performing a Live Show and Trafficking the Recording for Re-broadcast

For this case study, we'll look at another show that *isn't* pre-recorded, but performed live in the studio - we'll call this show "Live From Brooklyn."

The Problem:

Our host - we'll call her Sally - reports dutifully to the studio each Saturday at 2pm to perform her 2-hour live show, "Live from Brooklyn," to everyone listening to RFB live. However, not only do we need to find a way for MegaSeg to stop playing other shows while she's on the air, but we also need a way for her show to be recorded and then placed into the broadcast queue so that it can be re-aired throughout the week.

The Tools:

Audio Hijack (<u>https://www.rogueamoeba.com/</u> <u>audiohijack/</u>) Audio Hijack ($49) is another excellent product from Rogue Amoeba that allows you to record audio from any source on your computer. The software also has scheduling functionality, which is critical for what we need it to do in the studio, and one of the primary reasons we use it instead of other, free alternatives.

MegaSeg

Hazel

The Solution:

The first thing we need to accomplish in order for Sally to perform her live show, is to have MegaSeg stop broadcasting pre-recorded content so that Sally can get on the mic and do her thing. This is easily accomplished by simply creating an event, executed each week at the start of Sally's show, that inserts a "break" into the current MegaSeg playlist. A break is like hitting a "pause" button - it stops all playback and waits for human interaction (or in our case, another event) to get things moving again. To schedule the break for "The Live Show," we'd go to the Events tab in MegaSeg's settings, click "Create New Event," then "Insert Break" and schedule it to occur every Saturday at 2pm. Now all Sally has to do is wait for the break, and start her show. Inserting a break can also be a convenient way for our host to load up tracks she wants to play into MegaSeg before her show. Since the event simply inserts a break at the top of whatever current playlist is playing, but doesn't remove the playlist, the host can queue up her own tracks and breaks into the current playlist which she can play during her show by manually advancing through their tracks after the initial break is executed

The more challenging part of this case study is how to automatically get a recording of "Live from Brooklyn" into the broadcast queue for subsequent rebroadcasts. To do this, we'll use Audio Hijack and take the following steps:

1. Wherever you created your broadcast queue folders as described in the previous case study, create a new folder called "Live From Brooklyn" that contains two subfolders: "lfb-record" and "lfb-latest."

2. Open Audio Hijack and create a new session using "Input Device" as your source (figure 5-8).

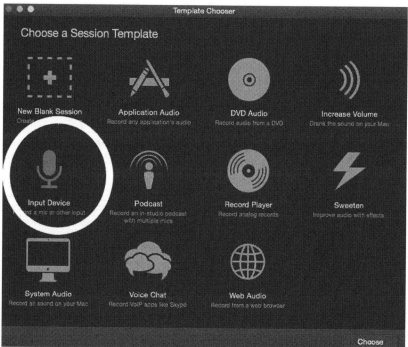

Figure: 5-8

3. Once the session is created, the input device will default to "Internal Mic," and you'll want to change this. Click

on the input device icon and select whatever device you use to get the audio from your shows into your computer. In our case, the device is called "USB AUDIO CODEC" (figure 5-9) as this refers to the signal coming into our Mac from the mixing board (see Chapter 3). You'll also notice that the default destination is an mp3 file set to 256kbps stereo. Depending on the bitrate allowed by your streaming host, you may want to adjust this as well. Since RFB's host accepts a maximum bitrate of 128kbps, we'll adjust this setting down to that bitrate so we won't get any loss in data when the show is re-broadcast (figure 5-10). As the destination folder, select the "lfb-record" folder within "Live from Brooklyn" folder that you created in step 1 inside the broadcast queue.

Figure: 5-9

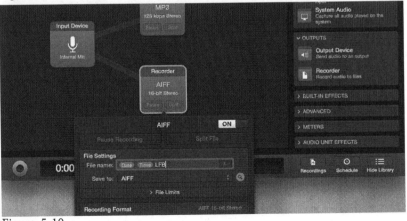

Figure: 5-10

4. Optionally, you can have Audio Hijack create a second file simultaneously. At Radio Free Brooklyn, in addition to the mp3 for re-broadcast, we have Audio Hijack create a hi-res (16-bit stereo) AIFF file with a destination folder that lives on an external hard drive. This is so we'll have an archive of hi-res files of all our live shows (figure 5-11.)

Figure: 5-11

5. Next, click on the "Schedule" icon in the lower right hand corner of the session window (figure 5-12.1), and then click "Add Timer" for the session you just created (figure 5-12.2).

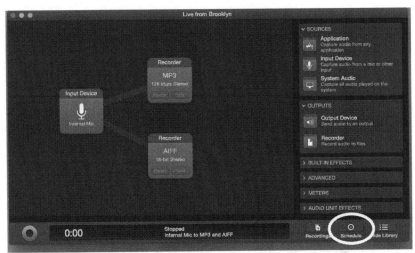

Figure: 5-12.1

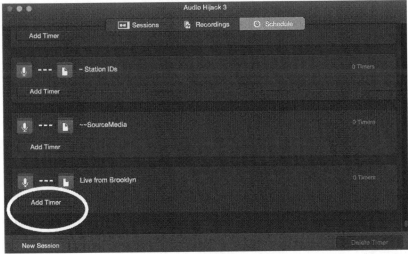

Figure: 5-12.2

6. Making sure that "Repeat Every" is selected in the drop-down menu, click on the day of the live show (in our case Saturday), then the start and end times of the show (2pm and 4pm respectively.) Leave "Quit sources when done" unchecked (figure 5-13).

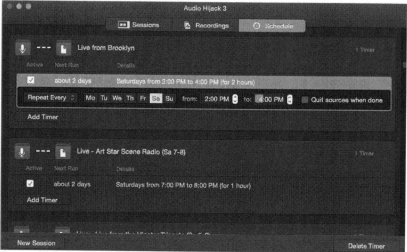

Figure: 5-13

7. Close the window, and return to the sessions tab - renaming the session you just created from "Input Device" to something that indicates the name of the show it's recording. In our case, we'll call the session "Live Recording – Live From Brooklyn."

Now we have Audio Hijack all set up to automatically record the live broadcast at the exact time of the show, but we still need to rename the file to our standard naming convention (lfb_latest) and make sure it overwrites whatever was in the queue previously. It may seem that the easiest way to do this would be to simply have Audio Hijack record the mp3 to the "lfb-latest" folder in the broadcast queue, but since Audio Hijack can't replace files (it will simply rename the file if another file is using the name specified), we need to find another solution. This is why we created a folder called "lfb-record" in step one, and why we had Audio Hijack record the mp3 to that folder. To get the file renamed and placed into the "latest" folder, overwriting any older file that may occupy that folder, we need to call Hazel back into action, using the following steps.

8. Open Hazel and add the folder "lfb-record" that you created in step 1.

9. Add a rule to this folder that will rename any file placed into it to "lfb_latest" and then move it into the "lfb-latest" folder. Make sure that in this second step you have selected "replace existing file" by clicking on the little info icon (figure 5-14). Finally add an action that will *copy* the file to the "LFB-ARCHIVE" folder in Sally's Dropbox show folder, and rename it with the current date (figure 5-15.

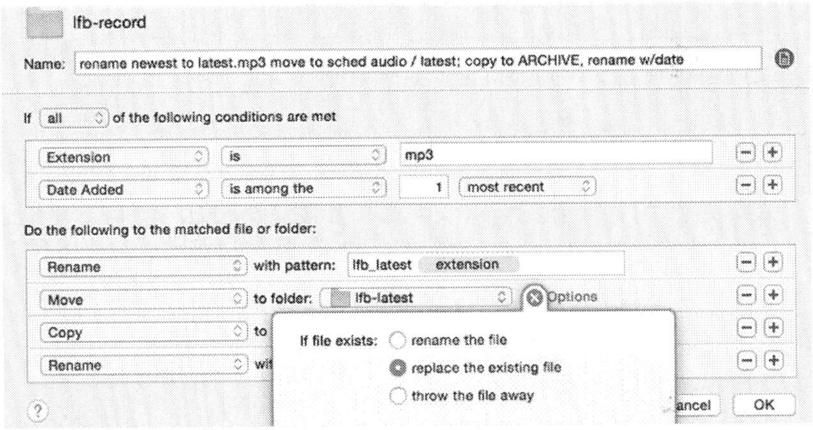

Figure: 5-14

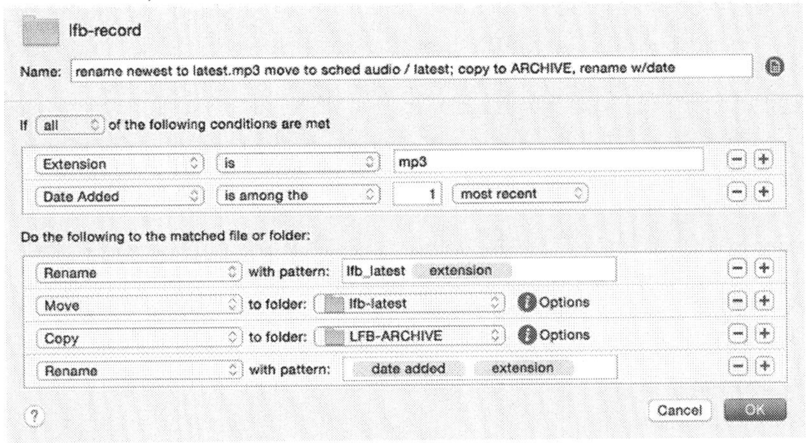

Figure: 5-15

If all these steps are executed correctly, your "lfb-record" folder will now be empty (file was moved to "lfb-latest") and ready to be used the next time Sally has a live show. Additionally, you'll have a file called "lfb_latest"in the "lfb-latest" folder ready to be picked up by MegaSeg for rebroadcast, which can be set up by simply repeating step 4 from the "Automation Protocols for Trafficking Pre-Programmed Shows" earlier in this chapter. Sally will also have an archive copy in her Dropbox folder and, if you chose to execute step 4 above, you'll have a hi-res AIFF archive copy for your station's library!

Case study: Protocols for Setting Up Syndicated Programming for Broadcast

Syndicated shows can be a great way to supplement your original programming with other shows distributed by other broadcasters and networks. These shows can often be obtained at no cost, either from the syndicated show or network's website, or though sites that aggregate syndicated content. A source for syndicated programming is listed in the Resources appendix at the end of this book. The main difference between syndicated shows and your original content when it comes to your internal protocols is that your syndicated content will have to be downloaded regularly, usually by accessing an XML feed. The good news is that there are many free software solutions that do just that, and we'll use one of the more popular ones, **Miro**, in this case study.

The Problem:

At Radio Free Brooklyn, we needed a way to locate syndicated shows, automatically download programming, and queue the shows up for broadcast.

The Tools:

Miro

Hazel

MegaSeg

The Solution:

Fortunately, finding syndicated shows, downloading episodes, and queuing them up for air is a fairly straightforward process - much simpler than the other two examples provided in this chapter. I won't delve too deeply into selection of syndicated shows (although there may be a chapter on syndication coming in future editions of this book) except to say that are a couple of excellent sites, listed in the directory at the end of this book, for browsing shows available to your station for free. Often the directories will provide a link to the XML feed for a show, providing you with a very easy way to access its programming.

Once you have identified the shows you'd like to air and obtained addresses to their feeds, you'll need a way to download them regularly and have them queued up for air. At Radio Free Brooklyn, we use a terrific open source solution called Miro that works on virtually any platform and can be downloaded for free from their site (http://www.getmiro.com) . Miro has a hugely diverse array of features and capabilities, but for this case study we're primarily concerned with its function as a "podcatcher" - a tool that automatically downloads podcasts and other audio content from an XML feed. Once you've downloaded Miro, the first thing you'll want to do - before you start downloading radio shows - is identify a folder to which Miro should download the episodes. If you don't take this step, Miro will download all episodes to its default folder, but you'll probably want to change this to a folder that you create within your Dropbox or broadcast queue hierarchies. Miro will then create subfolders for each show within the download folder you identify.

After you've set up your download folder, you can then start downloading your syndicated shows by copying the address of the XML
feed for the show, and selecting "Download from a URL" from
Miro's 'File' menu. Miro even saves you the step of pasting the URL
by automatically populating the URL field with any valid XML or
web address you have copied to your clipboard (figure 5-16.)

Figure: 5-16

Click 'OK' to start your download, and you should see your program show up in the "Podcasts" tab on the left hand side of the
window. Once you've imported your first episode, Miro will automatically download new episodes whenever they become available,
provided you leave the software running on your studio computer

Now that we know how to get syndicated programming onto your
computer, all that remains is to get it queued up for broadcast, and
for that we'll use a process very similar to the ones we used for our
original programming, enlisting the service of Hazel yet again.
Using a single show - "This Way Out" - as an example, the first
thing we'll want to do is create a Hazel rule that works on the This
Way Out folder within the Miro downloads folder you identified

earlier. Miro will automatically create and name a folder for this show (which it calls a "podcast") called "Series-Podcast--This-Way-Out" - this is the folder we'll want Hazel to act upon

Adding this folder to Hazel, our goal will be to create a rule that will be executed every time a new audio file is downloaded to this folder. The only condition we'll give Hazel is that the file must be an mp3 (which is the format of the downloaded audio) and if it is, to rename it to "two_latest," move it to a dedicated broadcast folder, and copy it to an archive folder for the show - exactly as we have done with the original programs described earlier in this chapter. Once again, be sure to tick the box in the options for the move action to "replace existing file" so that each "two_latest" file will overwrite the existing one in the broadcast folder.

The finished Hazel rule should then look something like the one seen in figure 5-17.

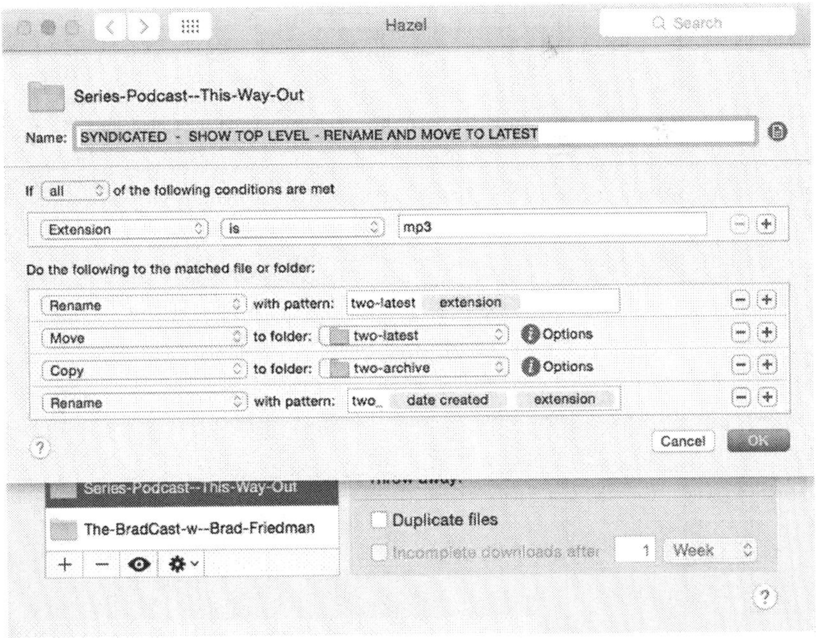

Figure: 5-17

The rest of the process for getting the show to air in MegaSeg at the correct date and time is no different than the process for original shows, i.e. import the file into a designated MegaSeg category before the first airdate, create a playlist, and then schedule that playlist to play weekly on the designated day and time.

In this chapter we've examined case studies for three processes that are the heart and soul of Radio Free Brooklyn's automation protocols. As I mentioned in the beginning of this book, you may need to tweak some of these depending on your station's individual needs, or your particular platform and hardware configuration. It's my hope, however, that by understanding the underlying logic, you'll be able to build out your own system for radio station automation and dispel any notions that you need "professional" radio automation systems that can run into the tens of thousands of dollars.

Chapter 6

Creating A Presence – Your Station's Website

Certainly one of the most important tools you'll need to consider when building an Internet radio station is the website. Your site, after all, is likely to be the number one destination for your listeners when they want to listen online, find information about your programming, or even buy merchandise that not only will bring a few dollars into your station, but also spread your brand with your logo brandished on t-shirts, mugs and tote bags. It's important to keep in mind that your website will most likely be the first impression your potential listeners will have of your station, so it's your job to seduce web visitors with a professional looking site where they can listen and explore. Your site should be simple enough that visitors find it easy to navigate and understand, but just complex enough that it's not boring. Regarding the latter point, in this chapter we'll look at ways of making your website dynamic enough that it will look a bit different every time a user visits, giving the impression that your site is an active destination where things are always changing, and not a boring static one that looks the same every time they visit.

Before we get started, it's important to note that the Radio Free Brooklyn website was built using the WordPress CMS (content management system) and that some of the examples given will be specific to that platform. However, as in the other chapters, it's my hope that an understanding of the underlying principles will provide you with an effective starting point for building your site, regardless of which platform you choose.

First, a few words about your logo.

Coming from the perspective of a long career in web marketing, I am consistently amazed at how often web brands either a) don't have a logo, or b) have an unattractive, hastily made, or non-communicative logo. By "non-communicative" what I mean is that your logo is a single graphical representation of your brand, so above all it should *communicate* what it is you do (less critical for large, established brands) and, more importantly, the style and personality you wish to convey. You don't *have* to spend a lot of money on a logo (or any money, for that matter, if you have friends who are talented designers), but if you're going to spend money on any single graphical element for your radio station, this should be the one you invest in. To give you an idea of what I'm talking about, here are a few examples of what I consider to be fantastic logos:

World Wildlife Foundation - The WWF logo is brilliant in that it tells us what they're about with a very simple design. After all, who doesn't love pandas (and wouldn't want to help this cute, sad looking one.) Simply put, their logo makes you want to give them money - WWF's primary goal - right after you give this sad panda a big hug, that is.

Nike - One of the most recognized logos in the world, the Nike design may not express explicitly what they do, but the simple swish does seem to imply swiftness and agility, perhaps due to its resemblance to the wings on the feet of the Roman god Mercury.

Toys "R" Us - This famous brand has the name *as* the logo, and there's no doubt that toys are what they do, indeed, it's who they "R". The font that's used in this logo also implies a childlike sense of fun, as do the colors (which unfortunately can't be seen in the black and white interior of this book.)

I hope these three examples help drive home my point that logo design should never be an afterthought, but a number one consideration when doing any kind of design for your brand, and that includes your website. All that being said, you don't have to spend a lot of money on logo design. If you're not familiar with the website fiverr (http://www.fiverr.com), it's an online community of artists, designers, technicians, and other talented people who will perform a variety of tasks and services, all at a single price point - five dollars. While finding a good logo designer on fiverr may be somewhat of a crapshoot, you may be able to identify the good ones by looking at examples of their work, and reading reviews by others who have contracted their services. After all, with a price tag of just five bucks, it's pretty hard to go wrong.

First impressions: Your home page

Although explaining the nuances of user experience and providing a laundry list all the reasons that good usability design are essential for your site (or any website) are beyond the scope of this book, I cannot overstate the importance of a cleanly designed, usable website in gaining fans and listeners. Your website, and more specifically your home page, is the first impression that potential listeners will have of your station, so it's critical that they are given a reason to stay, explore, listen - and then bookmark the page so they can return again and again. For this reason, it's important to put a fair amount of thought into your site before you start building, and the first question you may want to ask yourself is "what do I want visitors to *DO* on my site?" Although your specific goals may vary somewhat from station to station, the answer to this question for any radio station seems like something of a no-brainer -- you want them to *listen*! You may have secondary goals as well, such as wanting visitors to donate money, become sponsors, or like you on Facebook - but for most stations, listening will be the number one goal. For this reason, you'll want your player to be front, center, and bold. There should be absolutely no ambiguity or confusion about how one goes about listening - place the player on or near the top of your home page so it's the first thing visitors see when they reach your site. If you're using a pop-out player triggered by a "Listen Now" or "Listen Live" button, make the button red, yellow, or some other primary color that will leap off the page and grab the user by the eyeballs. Specifics on building an effective player will be described further in the next section, but for now I hope I've made my point perfectly clear - MAKE THEM LISTEN!

Before moving on, I will provide one caveat pertaining to this rule. Please, please, *please* do yourself a huge favor and resist the temptation to have your station "auto play" the minute a visitor arrives at your site. The reasons for this are innumerable, but the main one is that, on the whole, users hate it. Think about your own experience -- how many times have you landed on a website and immediately been blasted with music or, worse, ad content, that you neither asked for nor wanted? What did you do? If you're like me, you either immediately looked for the source of the offending sound and silenced it, or just closed the window or tab and went on with your web browsing, never to return to that particular site. One thing to consider about auto play is that the visitor might be listening to something else at the moment they arrive on your site and your content will interrupt them. They may also be working in a quiet office environment, and your auto play suddenly blasts out electronic dance music causing them the embarrassment of heads popping up from every cubicle like little corporate groundhogs to see who is suddenly throwing a dance party. I could go on and on - but I won't. Suffice it to say that auto play is simply a bad idea.

In addition to listening to your station live in real time, you may wish to entice potential listeners with some of the best previously aired programming from your archive. We'll discuss methods for archiving your content in the next chapter, but for now, you may want to consider providing a prominent spot on your home page for some of your best recent content. Often a visitor will come to your site because they are looking for a particular show - they may know the host or have read something about a particular program - so make these easy to find.

I've found that one of the best ways to lure site visitors into clicking that "Listen Live" button is to let them know what's playing at that very moment. At Radio Free Brooklyn, we provide a large, prominent, "On Now" module at the very top of the home page so that site visitors know what's playing at any given moment. However, building this module provided somewhat of a challenge: how do we provide "On Now" content that changes every hour or two, without having to modify the page by hand every time? For this solution, I'm going to provide you with one more automation recipe that utilizes tools that are readily available on the Internet.

Case study: Building an Automated Updater for an "On Now" Module on the Home Page

The Problem:

Build an automated protocol for dynamically updating home page module content that changes whenever a new show starts on the station.

> *The Tools*:
> IFTTT (http://www.ifttt.com)
> WordPress plugin: WP Latest Posts (https://wordpress.org/plugins/wp-latest-posts/)
> WordPress plugin: Redirection (https://wordpress.org/plugins/redirection/)
> WordPress plugin: Auto Prune Posts (https://wordpress.org/plugins/auto-prune-posts/)

The Solution:

The first action we'll take in this solution will be to simply create a blog post category in your WordPress installation that will identify posts to be displayed in an "On Now" module on your home page. Navigate to the categories list in the "Posts" section of your WordPress dashboard and create a new category. You can call it whatever you want, but for the purpose of this case study, we'll call ours "Now Playing."

Next, install an off-the-shelf WordPress plugin called WP Latest Posts. What this plugin does is simply allow you to create a home page module or widget that displays the latest posts for any given category. You'll want to configure the plugin settings so that your module displays only posts from the "Now Playing" category you just created, and limits the display to *only* show the latest post. There are also settings you can tweak allowing you to specify the height and width of your module, based on how large or small you'd like the "On Now" module to appear.

The next tool we'll explore in building out this automated module is an amazing little free web-based appliance called IFTTT (which stands for "If This Then That.") The basic concept behind IFTTT is that it creates actions for any number of different apps, software, or websites, which are triggered by conditions created by other apps, software, or websites. This is done by creating what IFTTT calls "recipes" which are essentially if/then statements using apps and websites as the triggers and actions. Heading over to IFTTT, we're going to create a free account, activate 2 channels - "Date & Time" and "WordPress" (you'll need your WordPress login credentials to create the latter channel.)

Now we'll create our first recipe. This will be for a show you'll want to appear in your "On Now" module at a specific time, so let's make up an example - we'll call our show "The Panic Room" and pretend that it airs every Friday at 1pm. We'll create our recipe for the show by taking the following steps:

1. Go to the "My Recipes" page and click on the big, blue "Create a Recipe" button (figure 6-4)

Figure: 6-4

2. Next, click on the word "this" which you'll see underlined, and in blue text (figure 6-5). This will take you to the screen where you'll identify your condition.

Figure: 6-5

3. On the next page, type "date & time" into the "Search Channels" box. This should make all the other channels disappear, except for "Date & Time." Click on this channel (figure 6-6.)

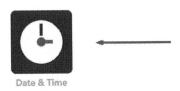

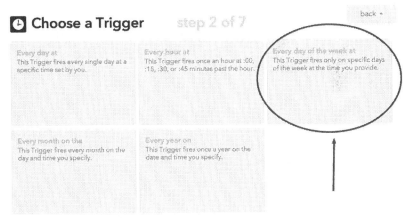

Figure: 6-6

    4. Next, you'll be asked to "Choose a Trigger." We'll select "Every Day of the Week at" (figure 6-7.)

Figure: 6-7

    5. On the following screen, select the date and time of the show. In our example, "The Panic Room" airs every Friday at 1pm. After selecting the day and time, click "Create Trigger" (figure 6-8.)

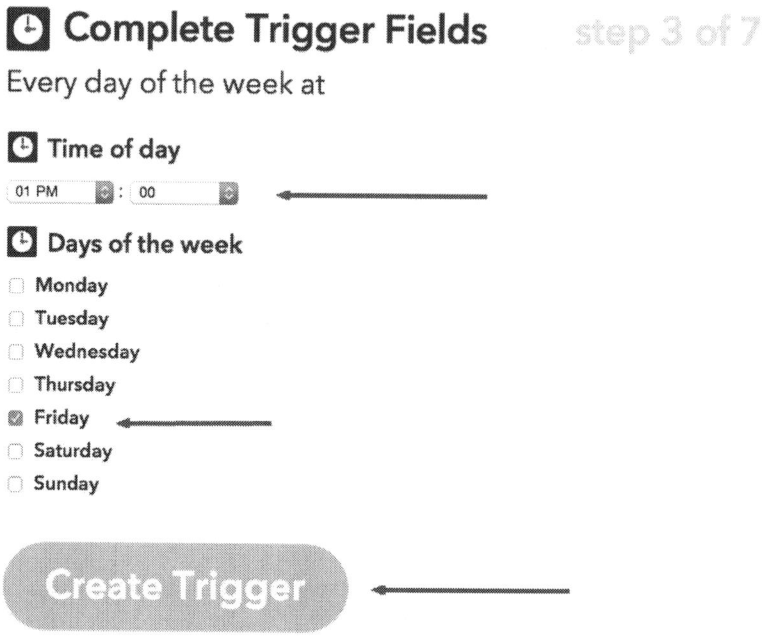

Complete Trigger Fields
step 3 of 7
Every day of the week at
Time of day
01 PM
00
Days of the week
Monday
Tuesday
Wednesday
Thursday
Friday
Saturday
Sunday
Create Trigger

Figure: 6-8

6. Next, click on the big, blue, underlined word "that" (figure 6-9)

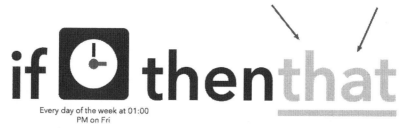

if
then
that
Every day of the week at 01:00
PM on Fri

Figure: 6-9

7. Now, we'll select an "action channel." Type "wordpress" into the channel search box, and click on the resulting WordPress icon (figure 6-10)

Choose Action Channel

Showing Channels that provide at least one Action. View all Channels

wordpress

WordPress

Figure: 6-10

8. On the following screen, we'll be asked to select a WordPress action. You have two choices: "Create a Post" or "Create a Photo Post." While either will work for our purposes, let's create a photo post (figure 6-11), since the show's logo will be the main content of your home page module.

Ⓦ Choose an Action

Create a post
This Action will create a normal post on your WordPress blog.

Create a photo post
This Action will create a photo post on your WordPress blog from the given URL to an image.

Figure: 6-10

9. You'll then be asked to complete the action fields for this post (figure 6-12.) They are:

a. Title - this will be the title of your post on WordPress. We'll call it "Now Playing: The Panic Room"

b. Photo URL - Here is where you'll enter the URL to the logo of the show that will be displayed in the module

c. Caption (optional) - You don't need to enter a caption, but if you'd like a bit of text under the photo you can enter it here. If not, leave it blank, but be sure to remove the default text, leaving only a blank box.

d. Categories - This tells IFTTT which category you want assigned to the post. Use the category you created in the very beginning of this case study. If you recall, the category we created for this example was "Now Playing." It's critical that you don't leave this field blank - and that you don't misspell your category - otherwise, the recipe won't work correctly.

e. Tags - Add any WordPress tags you'd like on this post. I recommend leaving this blank, since no one will be navigating to the post itself (we'll set up a redirect to the show page in the next step.)

f. Post Status - Select "Publish Immediately," if it's not already selected for you by default.

When you've completed all these fields, click the big, blue "Create Action" button.

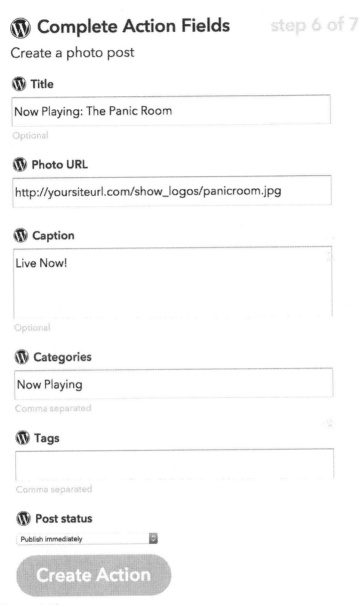

Figure: 6-12

10. Finally, you'll be asked to give your recipe a title. This can be whatever you like, since it's for your own internal purposes, but you'll probably want to give it a name that indi-

cates what it does. We'll call ours "Now Playing - The Panic Room." You'll notice that in my title (figure 6-13,) I've also included a couple of hashtags - #tpr and #live. Using hashtags in the title is a way to tag your recipes within IFTTT, so that you can find them easily. This will be especially important once you have several shows and need to filter them quickly to find what you're looking for. The two tags I've added indicate the name of the show (#tpr) and which airing of the show this recipe is for (#live) since I may want to create other "Now Playing" recipes for each time the show is re-broadcast. Finally, make sure you leave the box labeled "Receive notifications when this Recipe runs" *un*-checked - unless, of course, you *want* to receive an email every single time the show airs. When you're finished, click "Create Recipe" and you're done!

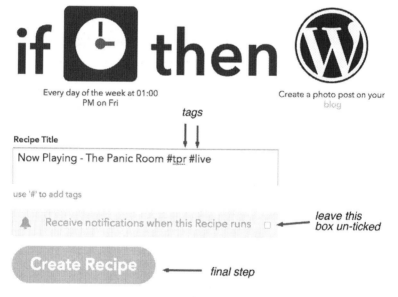

Figure: 6-13

At first glance, it may seem that creating a recipe for each show that airs is a lot of work, but once you've created your first two or three recipes, you'll be doing it in your sleep. After months of doing these, I estimate that each recipe I create for Radio Free Brooklyn, now takes me under a minute for each one.

Now that we've created a recipe to get content into the "On Now" module, we're still faced with a couple of challenges. The first is how to prevent people who click on the module from being directed to the post you just created - after all, it only contains a photo and a caption -- not exactly compelling content. I'd much rather have their click direct them to the show page for that show, and we can accomplish this using an extremely useful and versatile plugin called Redirection. The idea behind this plugin is that it redirects a web visitor who types in a web address (or in our case, clicks on a link) to another page on the site entirely. After installing the plugin, let's go to Redirection's settings and create our redirect. There are only a few fields we'll need to complete, and the first one is "Source URL." Here is where you'd normally place the URL of the page the user has entered or clicked on. However, since the IFTTT recipe will create a new page every time the show airs, it will create a unique URL each time. For example, the first time the recipe runs, it will create http://www.yoursite.com/now-playing-the-panic-room/ and the second time it runs it will create http://www.yoursite.com/now-playing-the-panic-room-2/ and so forth. To solve this problem, we're going to create a source URL with a wild card that will redirect every instance of the URL this recipe creates to the same place. This can be done in 3 easy steps:

1. Into the "Source URL" field, type: *^/now-playing-the-panic-room.*$* paying carful attention to the leading and trailing characters.

2. Making sure that "Match" is set to "URL Only" and "Action" is set to "Redirect to URL," check the box that says "Regular

Expression." Make sure this box is checked, as this particular redirect won't work without it.

3. In the "Target URL" field, enter the URL of the page you'd like the user to be redirected to, such a show page for "The Panic Room."

4. Click "Add Redirection" and you're done!

Now, every time a visitor to your site clicks on the "On Now" module, they will be redirected to the show page for the show that's currently playing. If you're using an SEO plugin, you may want to set it so that any pages in the "Now Playing" category are set to "noindex" so that Google won't list all of these pages that IFTTT created.

We're almost done, but we still have one little problem to figure out. If IFTTT is creating a new post for each show, each and every time they air, you'll quickly wind up with thousands upon thousands of posts that will serve no function once they have expired from the "On Now " module. To solve this issue, we'll use another WordPress Plugin called **Auto Prune Posts** (https://wordpress.org/plugins/auto-prune-posts/). What this does is allows you to set a time limit for posts in a certain category to live in the database, after which they'll be deleted. For the "Now Playing" category, I've set the plugin to delete posts after 36 hours (although this could feasibly be set much lower), keeping the number of posts to a manageable number.

Now that we've taken a look at some of the important home page elements, and created a dynamic module for displaying what's on your station at any given moment, let's move on to another important element of your site: the player.

Giving them what they came for: The audio player

Now that we've established that giving your website visitors a way to listen to your station should be among your top priorities, let's turn to strategies for getting an audio player onto your site. You have many options here, but we're going to focus on just two: an inline player that is embedded into your home page and will start playing with a single click, and a popup player that will launch a new, small window with an embedded player, allowing your visitors to continue browsing your site while they listen to your station. I'm going to start with the second option first, as it's my opinion that providing a popup player is the best way to encourage your visitors to continue listening while they continue to explore everything your site has to offer, and even allows them to continue listening after they've left your site

Creating popup players can be tricky, but one of the simplest ways to go is to embed a player from a third party provider that generates player code *for you*, and then simply use that code to generate your player page. At Radio Free Brooklyn, we use the player code provided to us from TuneIn (more on how to get your station into the TuneIn ecosystem will be provided in the next chapter.) To create the popup player on our home page, we simply followed these steps:

1. Create your player page: The first thing you'll want to do is create an html document that will contain the embedded player. In the <head> section, you'll add some CSS to make sure your code stays within the parameters of the window you'll define in the next step. So for example, by adding

    ```
    <head>
    <style type="text/css">

    body {
    ```

```
margin: 0;
padding: 0;
overflow-x:hidden;overflow-y:hidden;
}

</style>
</head>
```

you are telling the page not to add any extra room at the margins of the page, keeping it tightly within the size parameters you will set. Also, by having *overflow-x* and *overflow-y* set to *hidden*, you're instructing the page to clip any additional space that may overflow beyond the height and width of the page.

In the <body> section of the document, you'll first create a new <div> adding any style elements you'd like the page to have. For example:

```
<div style="text-align:center; font-family:verdana;
font-size:12;">
```

Next, simply paste the player code (ours is our TuneIn code), changing any attributes needed to ensure that the player fits the page. In our case, the player code exists in an iframe, and we'll change the width and height to 300 and 150 respectively, so that everything fits within the popup window. The result should look something like this:

```
<iframe style="width: 90%; height: 150px;"
src="http://tunein.com/embed/player/s246492/"
width="300" height="150" frameborder="no"
```

```
scrolling="no"></iframe><br /><br />
```

As you can see, we've also added parameters that tell the page NOT to add a border to the iframe, and NOT to scroll. We've also added a couple of line breaks after the player code to add some space between the player and the content below it. This could also be accomplished by adding a margin tag to the style element, such as *margin-bottom:20px;* The end result should look something like this:

```
<html>
<head>
<style type="text/css">

body {
margin: 0;
padding: 0;
overflow-x:hidden;overflow-y:hidden;
}

</style>
</head>
<body>
<div style="text-align:center; font-family:verdana;
font-size:12;">
<iframe style="width: 90%; height: 150px;"
src="http://tunein.com/embed/player/s246492/"
width="300" height="150" frameborder="no"
scrolling="no"></iframe><br /><br />
<em>Click the play button to enjoy Radio Free
Brooklyn's LIVE stream via</em> <br /><br />
<img src="http://radiofreebrooklyn.com/
logos/tunein_logo_150x32.jpg" style="max-
width:85px;"></div>
```

```
</body>
</html>
```

Save your html file, naming it 'audioplayer.html' or another name of your choosing, and upload it to your site.

2. Add a plugin to handle the popup: While you could write your own popup code using JavaScript, I'm going to make things much easier for your by turning you on to a plugin that will do all the heavy lifting, allowing you to use a simple shortcode [popup] wherever you'd like popups to appear on your site. The plugin is called Alligator Popup (https://wordpress.org/plugins/alligator-popup/) and since the options for the popups are entered directly into the short-code, there are no settings to configure after the plugin is installed.

3. Add the popup code to your site. Now, all that remains is to add the popup shortcode to either some text or an image. First, add the shortcode, including any specific parameters for the width, height, and scrolling of the new window:

```
[popup url="http://radiofreebrooklyn.com/
audioplayer.html" height="210" width="330"
scrollbars="no" alt="popup"]
```

Next, decide what the popup will link to (text or image) and add the code to display that. At Radio Free Brooklyn, we chose to link it to an image and text, so the code looks like this:

```
<img src="http://radiofreebrooklyn.com/images/
popup_icon.jpg" style="float:center; vertical-
```

align:middle;"> Popup Player

Finally, close the shortcode by adding: [/popup]

Here's what the finished shortcode looks like on Radio Free Brooklyn's site:

```
[popup url="http://radiofreebrooklyn.com/
audioplayer.html" height="210" width="330"
scrollbars="no" alt="popup"] <img src="http://
radiofreebrooklyn.com/images/popup_icon.
jpg" style="float:center; vertical-align:middle;">
 Popup Player[/popup]
```

And this is what it looks like on the Radio Free Brooklyn home page:

Figure: 6-14

Of course there are many other players available to you, as well as other methods of adding popups, but since this book is geared towards people who aren't developers or programmers, I wanted to provide the easiest, most straightforward solution available. For those who are feeling intrepid, however, I will offer another solution that allows you to build your own player and have it appear in a popup window, all with a single plugin called **MP3-jPlayer** (https://wordpress.org/plugins/mp3-jplayer/). This plugin has many, many great features including the ability to play directly from a SHOUTcast or Icecast stream, an interface to design your own player, HTML5 playback with fallback to Flash only when needed, an interface that works on both desktop and mobile devices, and excellent compatibility across browsers and platforms.

Now let's turn to an easier solution - embedding a player directly into a page or sidebar. Wherever your site visitor happens to be on your website, it's important that they *always* have the option of tuning into your station. On the home page especially, your player should live in a prominent position that the eye will land on within seconds after the page loads. At RFB, we placed the embedded player at the top of the page, directly below the main menu. In addition, we added the link to our popup player directly below it so that visitors have the option of playing the station inline or launching the popup so they can listen while continuing to explore the site. For the embedded player, we simply used the embed code provided by TuneIn, placing it not only on the home page, but at the top of the sidebar on secondary pages as well. This is simply a matter of adding a text widget with the player code to your page and post sidebars in WordPress. Some websites we've seen embed their player in a persistent "floating footer" at the bottom of the page which allows the player to stay in place from page-to-page so the user can navigate the site without interrupting the audio stream. This isn't a terrible solution, but it does come with the disadvantage that web users don't tend to look at the *bottom* of a page first, so it will take them longer to find it, if they find it at all.

Whichever method you decide to use, the most important thing is to make your player easily visible no matter where they are on your site. Every visitor is a potential listener and, in the long run, it's your listeners who create the greatest value for your radio station.

Make Your Hosts Feel Special - Give Them a Show Page!

Now that we've covered essential components of the home page, including an audio player and a "Now Playing" module, let's look one of the site's secondary pages that I consider to be a key element of any radio station's website: the show page. If you're like us, each and every show on your station will have it's own host, it's own sound, and its own personality. Diversity in programming is an asset to any station, so it's important to demonstrate the unique aspects of each show. Beyond this, and perhaps more importantly, every show will have its own listeners, its own *fans*, and they will want an opportunity to learn more about the host - including how to contact them or find them on social media - and to listen to archived recordings of the show. The show page is where you can make this all happen.

Creating show pages can be very easily done using WordPress native functionality - i.e. by simply creating website 'pages' in WordPress. This is probably the best solution if you are new to WordPress, or don't feel comfortable getting your hands dirty with simple coding. But if you're someone who understands a bit about how HTML and php coding works, you may want to investigate methods of creating a *custom content type* in WordPress. Custom content types allow you to create templated pages that only require you to fill out a number of fields on the back end, and will then assemble these into a page based on a template that you design. There are free plugins that offer relatively painless ways of doing this, like Pods (https://wordpress.org/plugins/pods/) - but at RFB, we like to use a suite of plugins called Toolset (https://wp-types.com/). There is a fairly hefty cost associated with Toolset ($149 for a year license; $299 for a lifetime license) but in my opinion, the lifetime license is well worth it, since you'll be able to use it on an unlimited number of sites - forever. According to their website,

> *Toolset plugins let you add custom functionality to any theme. Access the full power of the WordPress develop-ers API, without writing a single line of PHP.*"

While this is technically true, I will add the caveat that if you under-stand a little code, you will be much better equipped to handle all the incredible functionality that Toolset has to offer - and even then, there will be a bit of a learning curve.

The cornerstones of the suite are two plugins, called "Types" and "Views" - the former allows you to define your content types and custom fields, while the latter is designed to help you create tem-plates for viewing these custom types. When you're creating con-tent templates in "Views," a little HTML or php experience will go a long way in helping you tweak the look and feel of your template.

If you do decide to go the custom content route, the first thing you'll need to do is decide on the custom fields you will create to be included as part of your show page. In Toolset, these fields are created in "Types" and then assembled into a show page content template in "Views."

Without going into technical details about how to use these plugins - that would fill another book - I will give you an idea of the fields we created for our show pages, and give you an example of the output of the page template.

When considering custom fields for a show page, think about what you want your listeners to know about the show and its host. These are the custom fields we created for Radio Free Brooklyn hosts:

1. *Show name* (single line field)

2. *Show logo* (image field - hosts can upload their own show logo right from here)

3. *Live or Pre-recorded* (radio button -choose one or the other; the reason there is a field for this is that "Views" allows us to make conditional statements, so when creating the template, we can say "if the value of this field is 'live', then display the text "live on" before the show date and time, otherwise display "new shows on")

4. *Multiple Hosts* (radio button - yes or no; the logic behind this is similar to the above - i.e. if 'Multiple Hosts' is yes, display "About the Hosts" instead of "About the Host" in the heading for the host bio.)

5. *Host Name* (single line field)

6. *Host photo* (image field)

7. *Host Bio* (Multiple lines field)

8. *New Show Air Time* (Single line field)

9. *Show Description* (Multiple lines field)

10. *Podcast?* (Radio field; This fields asks the hosts if they have a podcast. If they do, then the next field becomes un-hidden, and they can enter the podcast URL)

11. *Podcast iTunes URL* - (URL field)

12. *Show Website* (URL field; This is in case the host has)

13. *Twitter ID* (Single line field)

14. *Instagram ID* (Single line field)

These 14 fields will all be filled out when you (or the show host) create the page by clicking "Create New Show" (figure 6-15). Taken by themselves, these data are just a jumble of information, so the next step before you can create this page is to create a content template in "Views" that will take each field and assign it a place on the page. When it's done, and you've created your first show, the result will be a fully formatted show page. Figure 6-16 represents what one of these pages looks like on Radio Free Brooklyn (with numbers representing the fields listed above.)

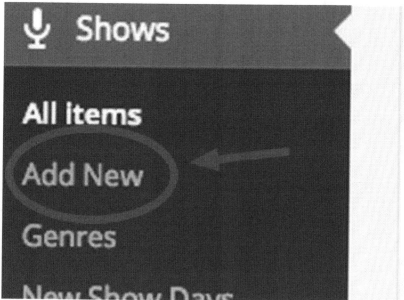

Figure: 6-15: Add a new show page just as you would a post or a page

Whether or not you decide to go with a solution for creating custom content types, show pages should be a major and easily-findable

Figure: 6-16: A completed show page

element of your website. I hope that the example provided here will, at the very least, give you an idea of the kind of content you might want to include on this page. Make your shows look good - your hosts will thank you for it!

Show 'Em What Ya Got: Adding a Weekly Schedule to Your Site

Another essential element to your website will be providing a schedule so your listeners will know what's on, and when to tune in to their favorite show. There are numerous free plugins that allow you to do this, but we want ours to perform a very specific function. First, we want the schedule to appear in a grid format, so visitors can get a birds eye view of what the weekly programming looks like, while still being able to easily locate what's happening on any given day and time. We also want to make the name of each program clickable, and take you directly to that show's show page when it's clicked on. You may also want the schedule to change each week so that non-weekly shows (such as shows that air bi-weekly, monthly, etc.) are also represented at the correct time.

One free option that looks very promising is a plugin called **Weekly Schedule** (https://wordpress.org/plugins/weekly-schedule/) that allows you to accomplish all of the goals above. The plugin is quite versatile, allowing you to set up your own schedule categories and day labels, link show titles to show pages, and also style the overall look and feel so that it integrates seamlessly with your web design. This would be a great plugin to use if you're launching a station with just a handful of shows, since you have to enter each instance of each show by hand.

At Radio Free Brooklyn, however, we launched our station with over 30 shows, and added 16 more just a few weeks later. Because of this, adding each show and rebroadcast by hand would quickly become a tedious, unwieldy task. After searching around for something that would make this a bit easier, we landed on a plugin called **Timetable Responsive Schedule for WordPress** (http://codecanyon.net/item/timetable-responsive-schedule-for-wordpress/7010836). While the plugin does come with a $19 price tag, it offers the convenience of adding multiple times for each live show or rebroadcast in a single entry. For example, if our hypothetical show "The Panic Room" (the one we created in the first case study earlier in this chapter) airs every Friday at 1pm, and then rebroadcasts every Sunday at 4pm, Tuesday at 9pm, and Thursday at 8am, I would have to create four separate entries if I were using the Weekly Schedule plugin. With the Timetable plugin, on the other hand, I can either create one entry for all four shows by simply adding airtimes to the show when I add it (figure 6-15). What we chose to do, however, was to create two entries for each show, one for the original air, and one for the rebroadcasts. By doing this, we were able to color code the shows so that live shows were in yellow boxes on the grid, pre-programmed shows in green boxes, and all rebroadcasts in gray. We're able to do this since each "event" allows you to change the background and text color, as well as provide a custom URL that the user is directed to when the name of the show is clicked, which in our case is the show page. When all the entries in your programming calendar are complete, your schedule should look something like what you see in figure 6-16 - with your own styling added, of course.

With the above examples, we've created some of the elements that are essential for any radio station website. Of course, you may have

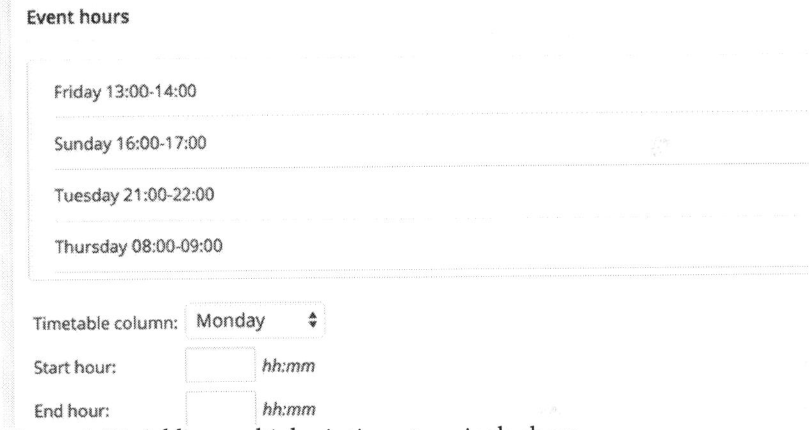

Figure: 6-17: Adding multiple air times to a single show

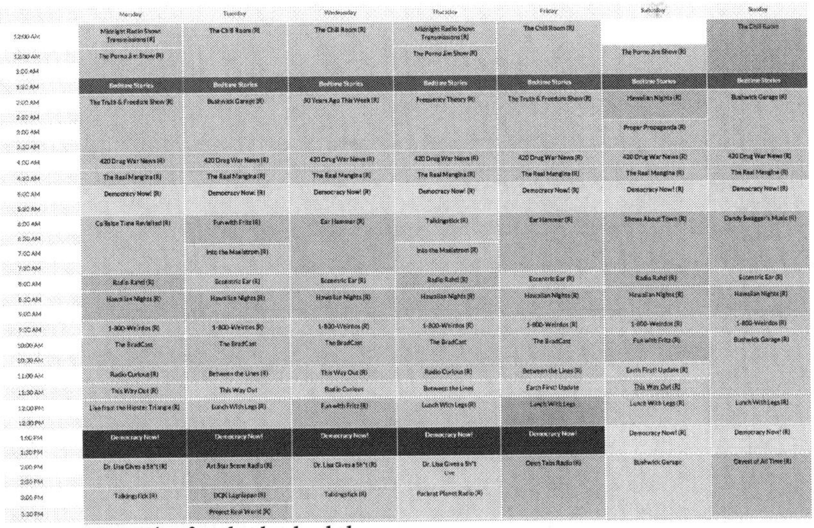

Figure: 6-18: The finished schedule

other goals you wish to accomplish with your site such as soliciting donations, obtaining sponsorship, selling merchandise, displaying photos of your studio, and showing off featured or recent shows and episodes. The WordPress website lists an enormous selection of plugins and other resources to help you accomplish many of these goals. You may have noticed that one of the things I *didn't* include in this chapter is a section about hosting the actual audio archives on your site. This is because audio files are large, and with multiple shows they can quickly add up to a size that your web-hosting provider may be unable to accommodate. This is a major reason that I always recommend hosting your audio files elsewhere - and that will be covered in the next chapter on content distribution. Before we end this chapter, however, I'd like to leave you with a quick cautionary tale that I hope will illustrate this point.

When we first launched Radio Free Brooklyn, we had all of our hosts upload their audio archive files to the website to be stored on our web server. We thought this would be perfectly ok, as our hosting package boasted "unlimited storage and data transfer" - so what could go wrong… right? Well, what we didn't take into account was that, while we did have the ability to store an unlimited number of files, after the files reached a specified capacity (in our case, 20GB), the host would stop performing automatic backups to our site. This would never even have come to my attention unless we had a need to quickly restore the site from a backup, which is, of course, what eventually happened. One late night a few weeks after launch, while working on the backend of the website, I accidentally hit the wrong button at the wrong time, and watched the entire website disappear before my eyes. I wasn't overly concerned at first, because I thought we could easily get back up and running by restoring from our web host's backup. I called tech support and they broke the very bad news - we had exceeded our 20GB limit, and no site backups had been performed. After screaming, yelling, weeping, gnashing my teeth and tearing my hair out, I quickly realized that all that could be done was the almost unthinkable task of rebuilding the site from scratch - which is exactly what I had to do. And it wasn't fun - at all. So, I end this chapter with a plea to each reader - DON'T DO WHAT I DID! Host your audio files elsewhere, and for goodness sake, perform your own backups - Every. Single. Day.

Chapter 7

Life After Airtime – Distributing Your Content

So you've got a radio station set up, your automation protocols are running smoothly, and you've even got a handful of listeners - congratulations! But your job isn't over yet. Broadcasting live or pre-recorded shows over the virtual airwaves is a fantastic accomplishment, but the life of these shows need not end there. We live in such an exciting time - whereas 20 or 30 years ago, a broadcast would have been relegated to a radio station's archive library right after its first or second airdate, the digital age we live in today offers fantastic opportunities to media programmers for giving life to media content for months and even years after it's first heard by listeners. However, it's important that you strike a balance between live listening and other distribution options - you don't want to sacrifice your station's listeners in the name of wider distribution. In this chapter, we'll discuss several methods of distributing your content without cannibalizing your live stream.

When it comes to content distribution, there are two basic methods we'll be discussing: placement of your live stream in as many places as possible, increasing the opportunities for live listening; and the distribution of audio content to audio aggregators and podcast networks after the original airdate. The first of these is the most straightforward, so we'll discuss it first.

Live Stream Distribution

Saying that increasing the number of locations from which your live stream can be accessed will increase your live listenership almost seems too obvious to mention. Since the meteoric rise of social media, particularly Facebook, occurred several years ago, businesses and brands are moving their web presence away from a complete focus on their websites, and more and more towards using social media sites and Web 2.0 technologies to "go where the party is." According to the latest Alexa Global Top Sites ranking (http://www.alexa.com/topsites), Facebook is the second most trafficked website in the world (right after Google), and YouTube and Twitter are both in the top 10. What this should signify for you as a new web radio entrepreneur is that you cannot rely the romantic principle of "if I build it they will come," but instead you must find out where the Internet radio party is happening, and put your stream right under your potential listeners' noses. In this section, we'll take a look at six of those places.

1. *iTunes Radio* - Besides being the dominant software for listening to your mp3 library, iTunes is also a major aggregator of Internet radio stations and is *the* destination for many Internet radio listeners. Although it can be a little hard to find - in the current version of iTunes, Internet radio can be found as the very last menu item under the "..." tab, next to Movies and TV Shows - once you're there, you'll find that iTunes offers an impressive selection of over 10,000 audio streams from stations around the world, with more being added every day. Fortunately, iTunes breaks these up into 25 categories, some with as few as 51 streams (comedy) and others with as many as 1,528 streams (religious). Clearly, if

you are a comedy network, your chances for discoverability in the iTunes database are much better than if you're running a religious station, since there are far fewer choices in that category. However, it's important to keep in mind that you *must* list yourself in the most accurate category, so don't choose your category based on the amount of competition. If, when applying for inclusion in the database, Apple gets the sense that you're being anything other than 100% honest, they can and *will* reject your station - and this may be permanent. Applying for inclusion is a very simple process, and will only take moments of your time, but there are a few strict rules that you must obey to the letter, or your station may be rejected. The following guidelines (in italics) are excerpted from Apple's official instructions:

- *Streams must broadcast at a bitrate of 128k or higher, except for spoken word such as News/Talk, Sports/Radio and non-music Comedy where 64k and higher are acceptable.*

- *Stations can list only one bitrate and one genre.*

- *Stations using names other than their own to be listed higher in the directory or twice in the directory will be rejected.*

- When you're ready to submit your station, your first step will be to download a submission spreadsheet from: http://www.itunes.com/radiosubmission. Submission requests must contain all of the following information and be submitted directly into the excel spreadsheet:

- *Station Name (this must be the name as it is used in your station's official branding; you may not change your name to start with 'A' to be listed higher unless it is a legitimate part of your station's name)*

- *Station genre*

- *City, State*
- *Country of Origin (select your 2-letter country code)*
- *Short station description (to be shown in tuner)*
- *Explicit material? (Yes or No)*
- *Frequency (select 23)*
- *Website for station (include full URL, beginning with http://www...)*
- *Approved (select Yes)*
- *Contact name, email, phone number and iTunes Store login account/email address*
- *Status (select Active)*
- *Strength (select 45)*
- *Audio Stream IP/URL (sorry, only one url per station)*
- *Language of Broadcast*
- *Commercial?*
- *Bandwidth Kbps (numeric value only)*

Please note that some of these fields may have been pre-populated in the spreadsheet for your convenience. When inserting information into the Station Genre, Country of Origin, Explicit, Frequency, Approved, Status Strength, Language and Commercial fields, please click the drop-down arrow to view your list of allowable entries. Inserting information that has not been made available to you in these fields will result in a rejected submission. Once you have completed your spreadsheet with all of the above required information, save your work and drop the excel file into an email with the remaining necessary station information attached directly in the body of your email:

Cover Art: attach a 1400 x 1400 JPG or PNG image

using RGB colorspace to your submission form.

Please note:

- *Stations will not be reviewed if they have not been submitted via an excel spreadsheet or have elements of the spreadsheet missing. All fields are mandatory*

- *Any spreadsheet that has been modified from the original template provided will not be reviewed or listed.*

- *Only one excel row per station.*

- *Our updated submission process relies on precise metadata. This means that any typos will result in an automatic rejection and the station owner will be notified and asked to review his or her spreadsheet for errors. Please review your station information for proper use of grammar and capitalization.*

Here are a few examples of station descriptions that will result in an automatic rejection:

- *The BEST Hits On The Air E V E R !!*
- *Beat Central –> Broadcasting Your Favorite Tunes !*
- *STREAMING HARDCORE HOUSE **24/7***
- *your official party station playing NON stop jams*

Here is how the above stations should read in order to be considered for approval:

- *The best hits on the air ever!!*
- *Beat Central, broadcasting your favorite tunes!*
- *Streaming hardcore house 24/7*
- *Your official party station playing non stop jams*

Once you have gone through this checklist, completed the Excel spreadsheet, and are confident that you've done everything correctly, all that remains is to send an email to: itunesradio@apple.com with the subject line (without the quotes:) "Station Submission: [your station name]" and making sure that you've attached both the completed spreadsheet and the 1400x1400 cover art graphic. You should receive a response within a few days, and if you've done everything correctly (and if the stream actually worked when Apple checked it) then your station should be accepted. Congratulations! You're now a part of one of the most popular Internet radio stream directories in the world, with access to millions of listeners!

2. *TuneIn Radio* - TuneIn Radio (http://www.tunein.com) is a hugely popular website and mobile app that boasts a database of over 100,000 streaming radio stations, and a listener base of over 50 million users in 230 countries - clearly a party you want to attend! The mobile app in particular has become the "go to" resource for listening to Internet radio on the go. Whether listening in a car, while jogging, on the bus, or just out for a walk, mobile listening has become so huge that at Radio Free Brooklyn, we estimate nearly *half* of our listeners access our stream using a mobile phone or device. Fortunately, adding your station to TuneIn couldn't be easier. First, head over to TuneIn's submission page at: http://tunein.com/syndication/new/?IsBroadcaster=true. From there, it's simply a matter of filling out a form of about 15 fields, including: Station Name, Email, Website, Stream URL, Broadcast Type, Country, Language, Format(s), Logo, Station Contact, Twitter ID, Phone Number, Slogan, Description and Comments. Sound easy? It is. One of the reasons TuneIn has become so successful as an audio content aggregator is that they make it *super* simple for stations to sign up. Once your station has been accepted, and

you've become part of the TuneIn ecosystem, you may see a sharp upturn in your listener numbers. The app's discoverability engine is one of the best I've seen, allowing you to browse "trending" shows and stations, search by locations and language, and find local radio stations with a single click. The app is also integrated with Facebook, so you can "follow" your friends and see what they're listening to, and the pro version even lets you record what you're listening to. In my opinion, TuneIn and iTunes are the two "must join" networks, and one of the major keys to your Internet radio success.

3. *Facebook* - As previously mentioned, Facebook is currently the #2 website in the world, so no matter what you may think about the site, or of social networking in general, it would be foolish of you to ignore the power of Facebook when it comes to promoting awareness of your station and gaining fans. Of course, you'll want to set up a fan page for your station, but did you know that you can place a live player for your stream directly on your Facebook page? A company called Radiojar (http://www.radiojar.com) has created a neat little Facebook plugin that allows you to place your live stream on your Facebook page, complete with a chat room to let listeners talk about your content as they're listening. However, due to Facebook's strict rules for apps, the player cannot be on the main page interface, i.e. the one with the timeline that your fans first see when they come to your page. Instead, it must be accessed using a tab at the top your page, but you can change the name of this tab in your page's settings from "RadioJar" to whatever you like. On the Radio Free Brooklyn page (http://www.facebook.com/radiofreebk) we use the simple call-to-action "Listen Live" so that visitors will know exactly what to expect when they

click. The plugin is completely free, and to get started using it, head to: https://apps.facebook.com/radiojar-plugins/

4. *Streaming Radio Directories* - Some stream host providers, such as internet-radio.com, provide their own directories of stations. However, there are many other directories out there and it's worth your time to register your station with as many as you can. While they don't have nearly the volume of traffic of iTunes, TuneIn or Facebook, people looking for new sources for their daily listening visit some of these directories regularly, so they may provide a great opportunity to add some new folks to your growing stable of fans. Some directories that you may wish to list your station with are:

   a. **Streema** (http://www.streema.com) - With a database of over 70,000 radio stations, Streema is an extremely popular Internet Radio Directory designed to facilitate both listening and sharing with your social networks. They also have free apps for iOs and Android users, making it easy to listen on mobile devices.

   b. **Reciva** (http://www.reciva.com) - Reciva provides access to a diverse range of Internet radio stations from around the world, with broadcasts from nearly every country on the planet. They provide both live and on-demand content and support RealAudio, Windows and mp3 streams. Reciva also syndicates their list out to many portable Internet radio devices.

   c. **StreamFinder** (http://www.streamfinder.com) - Steam-Finder is a free directory helping listeners find great streaming radio from around the world while helping streaming radio stations to promote themselves and gain more listeners. Their database contains roughly 13,000 radio stations, provides stats of users who find and visit your station, and while all services for broadcasters are free, for $10 a month you can become a "sponsor station" which gets you a listing on their homepage, a top listing on the genre pages of your choice and a listing in their mobile device directory.

d. **SHOUTcast Internet Radio Directory** (http://www. shoutcast.com/) - This is a directory of radio stations that use a SHOUTcast server, so unfortunately if you use Icecast, you're out of luck. The good news for SHOUTcast users is that anyone on a SHOUTcast server set to "public" should automatically be listed in their directory with no action required on your part. The directory lists over 60,000 stations, is very easy to search or browse by genre, and provides detailed info on each station about their listener numbers, bitrate, and type of stream used (MP3, AAC, etc.)

e. **Streamdir** (http://www.streamdir.com/) - Streamdir is a bare bones, very easy to use directory that allows broadcasters to add a station to their database in under a minute.

f. **Dirble** (http://www.dirble.com) - Dirble is yet another directory of streaming radio stations. Adding your station is very simple, and provided your stream is up and running when you submit, your listing will appear in seconds.

These six directories barely scratch the service compared to the number of directories on the web available to you to list your station. A simple Google search of "Internet Radio Directories" will yield almost 2 million results, so pour yourself a cup of coffee and get busy listing!

5. *Strategic Partnerships* - Before closing this section, I'd like to briefly explore an option available to you as a broadcaster that may not seem as obvious as those listed above. At Radio Free Brooklyn, one of the ways we've been able to get our stream "out there" on other websites is to create strategic partnerships with other organizations with whom we can forge a mutually beneficial relationship. For example, we were approached by a local events website called doNYC (http://www.donyc.com) that hosts a massive database of music, comedy, burlesque, and myriad other types of events in and around New York City. We were in need of a way to curate our own list of events on our site, and they were looking for sites like ours who needed a robust events database to power their own events calendar. It was a perfect match, and part of the deal we were able to work out with them was that they would host a player for our station on their site, giving us access to millions of potential listeners who lived in the area. We also agreed to let them host an events program on Radio Free Brooklyn, which will premiere in the fall of 2015. It was win/win all around. You don't need to wait for other organizations to contact you - be proactive and reach out to those who you think would be a good fit for your station. Remember, you're now running a media company and have a platform that may be enormously valuable to others.

Audio Aggregators and Podcast Networks

Working with audio content aggregators and podcast networks is not only a terrific way to give your station's content a long life after it originally airs, it can also be a great solution for hosting those hefty audio files that will weigh down your website as your library grows. Unless you've been living under a rock for the past 15 years, you know that iTunes is by far the largest podcast network in the world, and with over 800 million iTunes users and Apple's "Podcasts" app built into every iPhone, virtually everyone has these podcasts at their fingertips. What you may not know is that, due to licensing restrictions (more on licensing in the next chapter) it is *very* difficult to get a music podcast approved by Apple. The good news is that there are several other options available, and at Radio Free Brooklyn, we decided to go in two different directions for our archiving our content, using audioBoom and iTunes for our talk content and Mixcloud for music. They all provide opportunities to feature the archived content on our website, and are described below, along with a few other options you may wish to consider

1. *audioBoom* (http://www.audioboom.com) - audioBoom began its life as a simple mobile app called audioBoo, which allowed users to record and post short snippets of audio content using their mobile phones. Today, audioBoom has grown way beyond this limited functionality, and now describes itself as "*the leading mobile, web and connected device platform for the very best spoken-word content in news, current affairs, business, entertainment and sports.*" What they can provide for you, an Internet radio broadcaster, is a platform to upload your audio content and have it available not only to their own community of listeners, but to your website visitors as well, using their very user-friendly embeddable players. For broadcasters, audioBoom will set up a channel for your station that includes sub-channels for each of your shows. Each channel and sub-channel has its own RSS feed and shows can be submitted to iTunes for inclusion in their podcast directory in a few simple steps.

While the embeddable players can be used to showcase single episodes on your site, the RSS feeds can also be used to power an archive of *all* show content, should you decide to go with a podcast/audio player on your site that is able to pull in rich media from an RSS feed. You can also use audioBoom's RSS feeds to bring your shows into Stitcher, a service described later in this section. As if all this weren't enough, audioBoom provides stats and analytics for each of your channels, letting you look at total plays, top shows, listener demographics, and much more. The best part is that it's all entirely free for broadcasters. To get started as a broadcaster with audioBoom, head over to: https://audioboom.com/about/for-broadcasters to read about all the features available, then email them at pro@audioboom.com to get set up. Before we move on, one caveat bears mentioning - because of the licensing issues mentioned above, audioBoom only supports spoken word content at this time. For music content, we use Mixcloud, and we'll look at that next.

2. *Mixcloud* (http://www.mixcloud.com) - Mixcloud is a free service that allows radio stations and DJs to upload their shows and mixes, making them instantly available to its massive user base of online listeners, who can share them across social networks. Mixcloud's primary focus is online radio, so unlike audioBoom, who only host talk shows, Mixcloud not only supports music shows, they encourage them. Mixcloud addresses licensing issues by having their own blanket agreements with music publishers, and actually pay your royalties for you, so that the music artists get paid every time someone listens to your show. Like audio-Boom, Mixcloud offers embedded players that can live on your own website, offering your audience access to your

archived shows in a very attractive, customizable player. You can create embeddable "streams" for individual shows by creating a "playlist" for each of your shows, and then using the embeddable player for the playlist on your site's show page. By connecting your station's Facebook page and Twitter account, Mixcloud can automatically inform your fans every time a new show is uploaded. While basic membership is free and includes unlimited uploads, there is a "Pro" version with a monthly cost of $15, that provides you with profile customization, full statistics, scheduled uploading, and the ability to disable commenting, highlight content, make some content unlisted, and hide statistics. As with audioBoom, there are a couple of caveats to consider when choosing Mixcloud, both due to licensing restrictions. The first is that, due to the licensing deals in place with the publishers, Mixcloud does NOT support downloading of content, so your listeners will have to listen online, either on Mixcloud's site or yours. The second is that, because they must report the number of "plays" for each track in a radio show, Mixcloud players do not allow you to "rewind" while you listen, meaning you can't scrub backwards to listen to a song over again, although you can fast forward through a show. Even with these restrictions, we've found that Mixcloud is an excellent way to go as a solution for hosting our archived music shows.

In addition to these two solutions, there are a number of others that are worth mentioning and that may be of interest to you, depending on your individual needs.

3. *Soundcloud* (http://www.soundcloud.com) - Soundcloud is similar to Mixcloud, and describes itself as "the world's leading social sound platform where anyone can create

sounds and share them everywhere." Unlike Mixcloud, you'll need a Pro account ($6 or $15/month) to see stats on your listeners, and free accounts are limited to 180 minutes of music. The only way to get unlimited uploads (which Mixcloud offers even for free accounts) is to upload to a "Pro Unlimited" account for $15 per month. Also, since Soundcloud does not have licensing deals in place with publishers, they don't officially condone uploading of any content for which you don't hold the copyright. On the plus side, Soundcloud does support downloading of audio tracks, has several excellent embeddable audio players, and has a huge user community who regularly comment on each other's mixes and shows.

4. *Spreaker* (http://www.spreaker.com) - Spreaker is a podcast hosting network designed more for individual podcasts, less for full-time broadcasters such as yourself. They describe themselves as *"the best podcasting platform allowing you to create, distribute, measure, and listen to live, on-demand audio shows,"* and they may be just that, but their limits on the amount of audio you can upload vis-a-vis the cost of their plans, make it a less attractive solution compared to audioBoom or Mixcloud. For instance, their "broadcaster" plan, which will cost you $20 per month, only allows a total of 500 hours of audio storage. At Radio Free Brooklyn, we generate approximately 110 hours of original content per month, so this plan would last us less than 5 months. The next tier is $50 per month, which gets you 1,500 hours of storage, and the top plan features 5,000 hours of storage at a whopping $120 per month. Obviously, this cost is out of the realm of possibility for a small station like ours. One major benefit to using Spreaker, however, is that they have integrated their platform with iHeartRadio, a popular digi-

tal radio service, and Spreaker users can submit their shows for inclusion in the iHeartRadio database, but there is no guarantee of approval.

5. *Podomatic* (http://www.podomatic.com) - Like Spreaker, Podomatic is a podcast hosting network and is similarly geared towards individual podcasts, and not full streaming networks. They also offer a number of plans, the highest of which is the "Broadcaster" plan for $50 per month. This will get you 2TB of bandwidth (data transfer) monthly, and 20GB of storage. While both the bandwidth and storage may last you quite a while, you'll want to find something that scales as your network grows, and won't leave you high and dry once you've met your storage limit. At RFB, our music shows alone consume 100MB of storage for a 2-hour show, and with 10 music shows per week, we're generating 1GB weekly from music shows alone, and would run out of space on Podomatic within six months, even with their most expensive plan.

6. *Stitcher* (http://www.stitcher.com) - Stitcher is a bit different than the other services in that they don't provide hosting services, but instead uses RSS feeds (which you can set up using audioBoom) to pull your shows into its very popular app, which is used by millions of listeners on both iOs and Android devices. To have your shows syndicated through Stitcher, you'll need to fill out a very simple partner application form on their website. As with audioBoom and iTunes podcasts, it's unlikely that you'll get music shows approved on Stitcher because of strict licensing regulations, but they are a great option for distribution of your talk and spoken word content.

7. ShoutEngine (http://www.shoutengine.com) - ShoutEngine is a newcomer to the family of audio hosting sites and, as of this writing, their site is still in Beta. From what I've seen so far, however, the service looks like a very attractive alternative to those listed above, with unlimited storage and a pricing scheme that allows your plan to scale up depending on the specific traffic demands of your network. Each of their plans, including the free one, offers unlimited storage, and bandwidth allocation of 10GB per month for the free plan, 60GB for the standard plan ($10/month), and 180GB for the professional plan ($20/month). What's nice is that, for the standard and pro plans, you are allowed to exceed your bandwidth, and are charged the very reasonable rate of $0.10 per GB for any overages. The service boasts an infrastructure that spans 9 data centers in 6 countries on 5 continents to ensure that your audio content is always readily available. They also provide free analytics, an embeddable audio player, and RSS feeds that are "iTunes ready." While the newness of this service prevented us from signing on, it's definitely a site to watch in the future.

The solutions presented in this chapter represent just a small fraction of the distribution and syndication options available to you as an Internet radio broadcaster. With a little legwork and imagination, it's possible to find ways of getting your content out to listeners in ways not listed here, perhaps in ways that are yet unimagined. We're still in the very nascent stages of Internet radio and audio syndication technology, and I have little doubt that in the coming months and years, distribution options will continue to grow as new technologies emerge.

Chapter 8

Necessary Evils – Music Licensing

Regardless of what you may think of the state of American copyright law today, the reality is that if you plan on broadcasting music on your radio station, paying for that content is an issue that you'll have to contend with if you want your station to operate within the confines of the law.

While I'm sure there are numerous small stations out there that are "flying under the radar" - broadcasting music without paying for it - I *strongly* recommend that you not do this. The Recording Industry Association of America (RIAA) and many artists consider this to be piracy, and the RIAA has a history of being very aggressive when it comes to prosecuting individuals and organizations whom they perceive to be participating in copyright infringement.

Before we discuss ways of handling licensing fees for copyrighted content, I'd like to point out that, if you simply cannot afford licensing fees - which for small broadcasters usually amount to just over $1200 per year - you do have options for playing music on your station without having to pay for the right to do so.

1. *Play music you've composed yourself* - Any music you've composed yourself automatically makes you the copyright

holder for that composition, and as such, you are permitted to play that music provided it doesn't violate the copyright of another artist.

2. *Play music that uses a Creative Commons license* - If you're not familiar with Creative Commons (http://www.creativecommons.org) , you should be. They are a fantastic organization formed in 2001 which allows artists to attach licenses to their music, allowing others to use the work to sample, remix, and otherwise use their creation for the cultural good. Artists can choose a number of stipulations for their license, such as a rule that it can only be used for non-commercial purposes, so be sure to read each license carefully before you use the work. Soundcloud (http://www.soundcloud.com) and WFMU's Free Music Archive (http://www.freemusicarchive.org) are great places to find CC licensed tracks, and a full list of music communities utilizing these licenses can be found on Creative Commons' website at: https://creativecommons.org/music-communities.

3. *Use a streaming service that covers licensing payments* - Some live streaming services, like Live365 (http://www.live365.com) allow you to broadcast without paying for music licensing since they have blanket agreements in place with the publishers that cover all the broadcasters using their service. However, keep in mind that although you may not be paying for the rights directly, these costs are generally built into the service's pricing plans. Live365, for example, has three tiers of service. The cheapest is $39 per month, and includes 1,000 listener hours per month, which includes your live broadcasts and archived content, and only 4GB of audio storage. The second and third tiers cover 3,000 and 5,000 listener hours, provide 6GB or 8GB of storage,

and cost $109 and $199 per month, respectively. Services like this are great for part-time broadcasters, but for those looking to launch 24/7 streaming radio networks, they are impractical and expensive solutions. Another consideration to bear in mind is that services like Live365 only allow you to stream through their site, and don't provide you with a 24/7 live stream

Paying the Pipers: Music Licensing for Small Broadcasters

Music licensing can be a headache. Not only do the music publishers (ASCAP, BMI, and SESAC) need to get paid, but to stay completely legal, you'll need to pay for performance rights through SoundExchange as well. You will be required to keep careful records of every track that's played on your station, and be ready to submit complete reports when required. As a small, non-commercial broadcaster, there a couple of routes you can take to make sure you are in compliance with licensing regulations. The first is to pay for a service that handles everything for you (see option 1 below), or you can opt to pay the publishers and SoundExchange directly. Below are the options available to you as an independent broadcaster for making your payments and keeping yourself legit.

1. *StreamLicensing.com* (http://www.streamlicensing.com) - StreamLicensing.com is a fairly affordable solution that offers blanket coverage of all publisher and performance rights for a monthly fee based on your station's total listener hours (TLH) and revenue/expenses. The lowest pricing tier is $23 per month which covers up to 3,500 TLH for stations with expenses or revenue of not more than $20 per month. The way it works is that you must set up your site in a way that conforms to their specs, and they are able to automatically get track information for every track played, generate

and submit the reports for you, and pay your royalty and performance fees. On the surface, this looks like a terrific deal, but there are a couple of important points to keep in mind when considering using this service. The first is that in order for their system to get the requisite information for the publishers, you MUST set up your site to their specs and regulations. One of these is that your site's player must open in a separate page (popups are not allowed) that exists on *their* domain, making seamless design integration with your site a near impossibility. Additionally, they stipulate that as soon as the player page opens, the window for *your* site must close, making it impossible for visitors to browse your site while listening to your station. This is clearly not the best solution for a positive user experience. Another consideration is that one of the criteria for their pricing is how much gross revenue your station brings in OR how much it spends, seemingly making no distinction between the two. For example, if you are a small broadcaster with fewer than 3,500 listener hours per month, and spend approximately $100 per month on equipment, upkeep, etc. - your monthly cost will be $38.25. However, if you're not spending *any* money, but your gross *revenue* per month is around $100, you will pay exactly the same amount, $38.25. Surely there is some underlying logic to this equation, but I'll be the first to admit that it can be confusing at best.

2. *SoundExchange* (http://www.soundexchange.com) - While terrestrial radio (AM/FM) stations need only pay the music publishers for the music they play, streaming radio stations are responsible for payment to the producers and performers of the work as well. This is known as the "sound recording" copyright, which is usually owned by the record labels, and the collection and distribution of this compensation

has been entrusted to SoundExchange by the Librarian of Congress. For noncommercial webcasters, SoundExchange charges a flat rate of $500 per year per station which is *"credited against monthly liability accrued within the same calendar year. Services do not submit additional payment for that year until they have exceeded the minimum fee."* You will also need to supply SoundExchange with quarterly reports of all tracks played in the previous quarter, including track names, artist names, album, label, the ISRC number listed on the recording, and audience measurement for each performance. However, as an independent broadcaster, you may qualify for WSA (microcaster) status, in which case the reporting requirement may be waved, but you will still be responsible for the $500 minimum annual fee.

A SoundExchange license requires that you consent to the "sound recording performance complement," which states that:

- No more than 4 tracks by the same featured artist (or from a compilation album) may be streamed to the same listener within a 3 hour period (and no more than 3 of those tracks may be streamed consecutively); and

- No more than 3 tracks from the same album may be streamed to the same listener within a 3 hour period (and no more than 2 of those tracks may be streamed consecutively).

These rules are also enforced by Mixcloud, meaning if either of these rules are broken by a show uploaded to their service, they may remove the show completely or, as happened to me, make it unplayable in the

United States. These two regulations are important to remember if you're considering doing a show such as "A Tribute to Gwar" or any other themed programming that would necessitate the playing of a single artist throughout the entire show (or even a portion of a show.)

3. *ASCAP/BMI/SESAC* - If you choose to pay the music publisher royalties directly, you can simply go to each of the music publishing websites listed below and pay the appropriate annual fees. As an independent, non-commercial broadcaster, your estimated costs (as of August, 2015) are listed below.

    - **ASCAP** (http://www.ascap.com) - As an independent broadcaster, it's likely that you will qualify ASCAP's "Play Music" license, provided you have fewer than 30,000 monthly listeners, and a monthly revenue of under $2000. As of this writing, the Play Music license will cost you $288 annually. Reporting for ASCAP is due upon request.

    - **BMI** - (http://www.bmi.com) - BMI's rates for non-commercial digital broadcasters are a bit more expensive than ASCAP, with a minimum annual fee of $351 as of August, 2015. Keep in mind that, with BMI, they make a distinction between broadcasters who run "music stations" and those who simply play music on their station. The fee quoted above is for the latter, so if your station plays music 24/7, you may need to contact BMI for a more accurate rate.

    - **SESAC** (http://www.sesac.com) - SESAC is the third and final publishing organization you will need to deal with. In general, their rates are bit less expensive than ASCAP or

BMI, but the criteria for their rates are, by and large, even more confusing, and dependent on a number of factors. To obtain an accurate rate from SESAC, visit their site and obtain a quote based on information specific to your radio station.

Confused yet? If so, you're not alone. Music licensing is an arcane science, which, whether by intention or design, is seldom explained clearly in laymen's terms - and we're not quite through yet. There is still one area left to cover in this chapter, so grab a bottle of Excedrin and read on.

My Headache Just Got Worse: Reporting

In addition to all the hoops you've already been made to jump through just to get properly licensed, you may still need to generate quarterly reports of every track that has been played on your station for the past three months. Clearly, if you're running a 24/7 music station, this is a daunting task - a mountain of busy work that could easily consume most of your valuable time. As luck would have it, at Radio Free Brooklyn we stumbled upon a service that does much of that work for you. **Spinitron** (http://www.spinitron.com) is a web based service designed specifically for small broadcasters, that allows you to post your music playlists in real time, and then generate your reports whenever needed. The way it works is that each of your hosts or DJs are given a login to their website, and can build playlists from Spinitron's comprehensive music database either before, during, or after their show. An entry for any given track can include the track name, artist, album, label, year, length, and ISRC number. The playlists are then saved to your station's database, and reports can be generated when they are required. This solution removes a huge amount of work from your shoulders, and the cost for this service is a mere $50 per month for noncommercial broadcasters. In addition to Spinitron, there are a few other vendors, listed below, providing similar services and that may bear investigation depending on your specific needs. Please note that I don't have experience with the following companies - I provide this list only as a jumping-off point for your own research.

- *Triton Digital* (http://www.tritondigital.com/) – Triton provides reporting integrated within their own, proprietary streaming platform.

- *Backbone* (http://backboneradio.com/) – Backbone advertises a solution for "Online radio broadcast and automation for your Macintosh. They cater to non-profits, allow portable radio stations, and apparently offer a 30-day free trial, although we had a hard time getting anyone from their company to respond to our requests.

- *MusicMaster* (http://www.musicmasteronline.com/) – MusicMaster is music-scheduling technology that provides reporting as well.

- *PowerGold* (http://www.powergold.com/) – Yet another music scheduling service that features built-in reporting.

- *RadioActivity* (http://www.radioactivity.fm/) – Like Spinitron, RadioActivity is a web-based playlist logging service that also provides reporting. A very reasonable pricetag of just $400 per year makes this one definitely worthy of investigation.

- *Spacial Audio* (http://www.spacial.com) – Spacial is the company that makes SAM Broadcaster (see chapter 4), and their reporting features are integrated seamlessly with SAM. If you run your system on Windows, this may be a good way to go.

- *Surfer Network* (http://www.surfernetwork.com/) – Surfer Network caters to mid and small markets. They offer a complete streaming platform that advertises "SoundExchange reporting in just a couple of clicks."

- *StreamAudio* (http://firststreaming.com/) – StreamAudio provides stream hosting services with an integrated reporting package.

As you can see, there are numerous options available when it comes to music reporting. At RFB, we went for an option that was low-cost and catered to our particular niche (noncommercial, community webcasters), but you may choose an entirely different direction depending on your own business model and goals. If you have experiences to share with any of the services listed above, please share them with me via the email address provided in the introduction, as I'd love to keep this chapter updated for future editions of this book.

Chapter 9

Strutting Your Stuff – Promoting Your Radio Station

By this point, I hope this book has given you a good idea of all the work that goes into creating a live 24/7 streaming radio station. You've established goals, set yourself up with a streaming host, assembled a studio, created automation systems, built a website, investigated ways of distributing your content, and obtained licenses to stream your music. Wow, you've been busy! But the work isn't over, you still need the key ingredient necessary for any successful radio station -- listeners.

After your station is up and running, every thought during every waking hour of your day should be guided by the question: *how can I get more people to listen?* If you're like me, promoting your station will be the fun part of your job, although like all the rest, it still requires a lot of hard work and creative thinking. The strategies and tactics I will describe in this chapter are just a few that we've used at Radio Free Brooklyn, but it's important to remember that means of promotion are limited only by your imagination. In fact, the more imaginative and creative you get with your promotional strategies, the more your station will cut through the noise and stand out from all the others.

Think carefully about your demographic. Who are the people you want listening to your station? How old are they? What do they like to do (besides listen to the radio?) Where do they hang out? Are they already Internet radio listeners, or will you have to change their habits? Do they use social media, or are they more of an old-school email crowd? If you're like many people, your first reaction to the question *"who?"* might be, *"everyone!"*

While it would certainly be nice to have "everyone" listen to your station, the fact is that your listeners are likely to fall into a certain age group with a specific set of interests, and when you understand who these people are, you'll be able to make your promotional strategies far more targeted and effective. For that reason, it's very important that you're able to be flexible in executing some of these recommended strategies, adapting them to the demographic you envision for your station.

Some of the tactics below - such as media partnerships, merchandise, and live events - may overlap somewhat with the income strategies I outlined in Chapter 1, and that's as it should be. There's no reason that your promotional strategies shouldn't have a money-making component, just as there's no reason you can't use income strategies to promote your station. In fact, the more ways you can find to do both at the same time, the faster your station will grow.

Before we dive into the list, I want to offer one last bit of advice regarding listener numbers. When you first launch your station, your listener numbers *will* be low. Don't be discouraged by this, and certainly don't obsess over it. Success rarely happens overnight, and just about every successful business starts off slow, eventually *becoming* a success with a lot of attention and hard work. In fact, when I was creating the business plan for my first business back in the early 90's, my attorney at the time advised me to "plan on zero income for the first 18 months." This was, perhaps, the best business advice I've ever received, as it required me to prepare for the worst, and made me ready to tough out those rough first several months. If you're running a station with a number of different hosts and DJs, I can almost guarantee that many of them will ask you for their listener numbers, often after only having done a show or two. Try to resist the temptation to share numbers right away, as this may only end up discouraging your hosts, especially if they've never done a radio show before. Instead, consider utilizing a tactic such as creating leaderboards (described later in this chapter) to show where they are ranking compared to their peers.

You, as the station owner, will *have* to dig into your numbers from time to time over the first few months - when you're estimating listener hours for music licensing, for example - but I implore you to not let low numbers discourage you. Trust your gut. If you're on the right path, you'll know it, and you *will* be successful in the end.

The promotional tactics that follow are ranked in order from the simplest to the most complex, so you should by no means feel that you have to accomplish them in any particular order. Some of them you may not want to try at all, while others may spark an idea for another tactic altogether. These are methods that have worked for us, and hopefully will be helpful to you in developing your own promotional strategy. Have fun!

1. *Station IDs* - This tactic is so simple that it may seem self-evident, but I'll share it just the same. Whether your hosts and DJs are performing live shows or sending in pre-recorded content, make it a policy that all shows broadcast over your network provide station IDs at least every 15 minutes or so. A station ID is simply the host saying something like *"You're listening to The Panic Room on XYZ Radio."* Doing this

accomplishes two important goals. First, it reminds listeners of which network they're listening to, further embedding your brand name into their consciousness. Secondly, and perhaps more importantly, if someone is listening after the original airdate, on a podcast for example, it lets him or her know where the content originated. If they like the content enough, they may become avid listeners! Also, if you ever have someone famous (or even semi-famous or locally-famous) as a guest in your studio, make sure to have him or her record a station ID. Can you imagine how much cred you'd gain if you had *"Hey this is Mick Jagger, and you're listening to XYZ Radio!"* playing every hour between shows? (Ok, I get that Mick Jagger is a pie-in-the-sky example, but you get the idea.) I perform a music show live every Wednesday evening, and I *always* make sure that my show begins and ends with one of the celebrity station IDs we've collected. Having someone like indie rock star Mike Doughty or internationally famous Brazilian vocalist Bebel Gilberto begin my show by promoting my station adds an invaluable layer of credibility to both my show and my station. If a listener who is unfamiliar with RFB is tuning in on Mixcloud, for example, hearing this celebrity endorsement may help turn him or her into a regular listener.

2. *Stickers* - When my partner, Rob, first suggested that we get RFB stickers made up, I was skeptical. I was unsure how much promotional value we'd get from these little pieces of vinyl with sticky backs on them. However, I quickly discovered that stickers are *great* for garnering grassroots brand awareness. First of all, most people apparently still nurture an inner 10-year-old that just loves to peel and stick things wherever they can, and this can certainly work to your advantage. After giving away a few thousand stickers

at our launch party, at the bike shop that hosts our studio, and by leaving them at local businesses, we soon found that they were popping up *everywhere* throughout NYC. I've even had people say to me, *"Sure, I've heard of Radio Free Brooklyn - I've seen your stickers."* Soon enough, our sticker meme expanded beyond the New York tri-state area, and started showing up in other parts of the country, and even in Europe and Asia. We now send out regular calls-to-action for fans to send us photos of their RFB stickers posted in public spaces (in a legal, non-vandalizing way, of course) around the world. Many of the pics are tweeted out to our fans, some are posted on our website, and it's become a fun way to involve our fans in a promotional strategy.

3. *Email Signatures* - Whether you use gmail, Apple Mail, Outlook, Entourage, Yahoo, or any one of the hundreds of others, Just about every email program these days has a way to insert an email signature into the end of your email messages. This is a very simple tool, but one that can be powerful when it comes to brand awareness. By way of example, my email signature looks like this:

Tom Tenney
Co-founder & Program Director, Radio Free Brooklyn
http://www.radiofreebrooklyn.com

While just about everyone that knows me knows that I am involved with Radio Free Brooklyn, this little snippet at the end of all my email messages *reminds them* of that fact, and may even make them think, *"Oh yeah... I've been meaning to check that out."* Conveniently, there is an active link in the signature, allowing to do just that with a single click. You should also encourage your hosts to include signatures in their emails as well. After all, the more your brand is in front of the right eyeballs, the more potential listeners you will have. This is a cheap, easy, no-risk tactic, so there's really no reason not to use it.

4. *Mailing Lists* - Having an opt-in mailing list is a fantastic way to keep your fans and listeners updated on what's going on with your radio station. "Opt-in" means that the subscriber *chose* to be added to your list, as opposed to you entering a list of emails without their permission (we *strongly* advise against the latter.) This way, you know when you send an email that you're talking to someone who is interested in what you have to say. We also recommend using an email list service as opposed to sending an email from your account and cc'ing hundreds of people, which is a good way to get yourself put on a spam blacklist. Most list services are free these days, and the options are innumerable, but we like Mailchimp (http://www.mailchimp.com). It's free, very easy to use, has several design templates that you can customize to your own look and feel, and provides something called "segments" with which you can section your lists into different types of subscribers. For example, you can have a "master" mailing list for your station, and segments of that list for local fans, sponsors, and partners. Each of these segments can then be emailed as a group, so they get messages that are targeted to them specifically, and won't have to read emails that are irrelevant to them. Mailchimp also offers a very easy way to embed a signup form on your website, turning each visitor into a potential subscriber.

5. *Business Cards* - Although they may seem a bit "last century," business cards are still a great way to represent yourself and your station, and a necessary tool if you're going

to be interacting with any local businesses on your station's behalf. One of the nice things about business cards is that, these days, they can be purchased for pocket change. For example, at Vistaprint (http://www.vistaprint.com) 100 full color business cards of your own design cost just $16. The vendor we use, MOO (http://www.moo.com) are a bit more expensive, but the quality is a little better, and their turnaround is very fast. At such cheap prices, there's no reason not to have business cards as part of your promotional toolkit.

6. *Social Networks* - There's no doubt that social media has become the 21st century's de facto method of grassroots promotion, and if you and your station are not a part of it, you're doing yourself a great disservice. Whether people are at home, at work, or out and about on their mobile devices, social media sites are how people stay in touch with friends, get their news, and just generally hang out. It's also an invaluable resource for you to get the word out about your station. I don't necessarily think you have to go crazy and join every network on the Internet, but you should, at the very least, have a presence on Facebook and Twitter, the two most popular social networks. Below is very quick rundown of the top social media sites, and how you might use them to promote your station.

    a. Facebook - As mentioned in Chapter 7, having a Facebook page is essential. Not only is it a terrific place to embed your live stream, but as you get more and more fans, they will start sharing your content, giving you exposure to an exponentially greater number of potential listeners. With that in mind, think carefully about what you share. Being selective and not sharing every single tidbit of news will go a long way towards keeping people interested in what you are sharing. After all, if you share *everything,* your fans are likely to get annoyed and "turn you down" in their feed, or worse, unlike you. When considering what to share, ask yourself, "is this something *others* will want to share?" Your most valuable posts will be the ones that others want to share with *their* networks.   At RFB, some of our most shared posts are those that are funny or contain valuable information. For example, many of our photos of RFB stickers in exotic places get circulated widely, whereas the fact that we just uploaded something to Mixcloud may not be. Be smart and strategic with your shares, and Facebook will quickly become your best promotional resource.

b. Twitter - Twitter, like Facebook, is an essential network to be a part of. While it can be a bit hit-or-miss as to who sees your posts, there are tactics you can employ that will keep you active and engaged, and ensure that your follower numbers continue to rise. The first of these tactics is the retweet. People love to have their tweets reposted by others, so make it a point to retweet anyone who either a) mentions you in a tweet, or b) posts something relevant to your station.   The second tactic is to engage in conversations on Twitter. Engaged organizations are *engaging* organizations. Respond to what others are tweeting about, start a conversation, show the world that you're not there just to hawk your station, but that your station is an active, enthusiastic organization that takes an interest in the community. Before long, you'll find you have turned many of those people you've responded to and retweeted into followers and, hopefully, listeners.

c. Instagram - Radio, by definition, is a non-visual medium. However, we live in a visual culture, where people like to be able to put an image to words. Instagram affords a valuable opportunity to show what the world of your radio station *looks like* - so consider posting photos that show the inside of your studio, perhaps candid photos of some of your live hosts performing their show, or even street photos you take on your mobile phone that speak to the brand image you're trying to build. The more potential listeners are able to represent you in their minds with visual images, the more they will remember you. And the more they remember you, the more likely they are to tune in.

d. Pinterest - Applying the same principals described above for Instagram, you may also wish to start a Pinterest account for your station. Perhaps you can start a collection of photos relating to the history of radio, or maybe one that shows other Internet radio stations like yours around the world. The great thing about Pinterest is that your posts aren't only seen by your followers, but can be discovered by the entire Pinterest community. This is a great way to garner interest in your station from people who may otherwise not even have known who you are.

e. LinkedIn - If you're already an active LinkedIn user, make sure that you have added your radio credentials to your professional profile. This, like Pinterest, is another good way of exposing your station to others who may not know you. LinkedIn also has several professional groups you can join - there's even one that's specific to Internet Radio - where you can engage in meaningful discussions while at the same time exposing your brand

7. *Leaderboards* - The hosts of your shows should absolutely be a part of your promotional team, using their own resources to get word of the station out to their networks. However, not everyone on your team will have the same mind for promotion you do, so here's a way you can jumpstart their engagement. Every week - or every month, whichever you think will be more effective - send an email out to all your hosts to let them know how their show is doing. Don't provide them with hard numbers, which may be counter-productive, but instead give them lists of the "Top 5" or "Top 10 " shows and how they are ranking with their peers. For example, at Radio Free Brooklyn we do "Top 5" lists for different categories - listener numbers, audioBoom listens, Mixcloud listens, show page visits on the website, and Facebook engagement for their posts (they are all able to post as Radio Free Brooklyn) which we can measure using Facebook's Insights analytics program. Human beings are competitive by nature, and even without seeing the hard numbers, seeing how they rank against other shows sparks that competitive instinct. Seeing these stats makes them want to do better than the others, and they'll start looking at what kinds of promotional tactics are being used by hosts of shows that rank higher than them and, hopefully, emulating those tactics. This strategy isn't guaranteed to work on everyone, but we've seen good results with it so far at RFB.

8. *Merchandise* - This is another topic that was discussed early in this book, but it bears revisiting because merchandise isn't just a way to make money, it's a way to get your

brand out into the world. If you have a strong logo (more on logos can be found in Chapter 6) then you should be leveraging that strength in every way you can. People love swag, and often don't mind paying for it if it's a cool brand that will bump up their own "cool factor" by wearing it. And as the brand owner, there will be nothing more thrilling than passing someone on the street who is wearing a t-shirt or hat emblazoned with your radio station's logo. At Radio Free Brooklyn, we use our website and live events to sell t-shirts, tank tops, hats, coffee mugs, tote bags, and sweatshirts. Now, you may be asking yourself, *"But what if it doesn't sell? I can't afford to lay out money up front for merch that may or may not sell!"* This is where I have some excellent news - you don't have to lay out a dime. Thankfully, there are a number of "print on demand" services that will print your products on an as-needed basis. In other words, first you sell the product, then the product is printed and shipped. The service we use at RFB is a company called **Printful** (http://www.theprintful.com) and they print a number of quality products at excellent rates. The best part is that Printful integrates seamlessly with a large number of ecommerce packages (we use **WooCommerce**) so that the user never leaves your site, nor do they even know that there is another party fulfilling their products. When orders are sent out to your customers, Printful will even customize their mailing label with your station's name and logo, and the customer is never the wiser. I'll give you an idea of how this works with a simple example. A fan of your station - we'll call her Marjorie - orders a t-shirt on your website, and receives an email confirmation that her order has been received. Behind the scenes, Printful receives this order, including color and size, prints it up and sends it out to Marjorie within a day or two. Marjorie is billed $25 for the shirt, which goes to you, and you are billed $13.00 for the shirt with a credit card kept on file with Printful. The difference, $12, is the profit, and is yours to keep. Obviously, you will need some merchandise in inventory if you're going to sell at live events, but these can be purchased at cost from Printful, and there's no minimum quantity so you can order only as much as you need. I should also mention that in order to use a service like WooCommerce on your site, you will need to have a payment gateway which you can get for under $10 per month. Options are listed in the Resources section at the end of this book.

9. *Events* - Producing live events is always a great promotional tactic, although it does take some legwork as well as modicum of producing know-how. The type of event you choose to produce should be dictated by the type of radio station you are. If you are a 24/7 music station featuring the best in indie music, why not produce an indie music showcase in your city? If you stream only hip-hop, host a DJ battle. If you're an "all comedy, all the time" network, it would make sense to produce a stand up showcase, or an improv battle. One great thing about having a radio station is that most performers, particularly musicians, are excited to be a part of something that involves them with mass media, no matter how small that media outlet may be. If you're able to live broadcast the event, even better because not only does everyone love to hear themselves on the radio, but if the artists are performing on a broadcast that's available worldwide, they are likely to tell their friends and family to tune in, no matter where they're located. Another type of event you may wish to consider is one that is a purely promotional play. In October of 2015, Radio Free Brooklyn will be hosting a month-long, borough-wide scavenger

hunt. Participants will need to tune in to RFB programs to find out where to get the next clue, and then patronize a local business to get the clue itself. The prize is a brand new bicycle from the Velo Brooklyn Bike Shop, which is where our studio is located, and will be awarded to the lucky winner at an RFB fundraising event at the end of the month. There will also be smaller prizes awarded along the way, and these will be provided by event sponsors, as well as by the local businesses themselves. While we will be shelling out approximately $500 for the grand prize, we'll be getting promotional value that far exceeds that amount. First of all, since contestants will have to listen to our shows to learn where to get clues, they will automatically be exposed to our programming. Some may not stick around after the contest as regular listeners, but some may, and the ones that do will hopefully become evangelists for our brand. Additional value can be found in the forging of relationships with local businesses. RFB is a community organization, and working with independent businesspeople on a fun event such as this will hopefully pave the way towards even more fruitful relationships in the future. Events like these have many moving parts, and are not easy to produce, but if you've got the time, talent, and inclination, they can be real showstoppers when it comes to promotional value.

10. *Media Partnerships* - Finally, I would like to revisit, briefly, the idea of media partnerships I touched on in Chapter 1. As the owner of an independent media outlet, you possess something of great value not only to you, but also to many others in the community. One of the most difficult challenges for any small business or organization is figuring out how to "cut through the clutter" and get your message heard. Big media is, for all practical purposes, an inaccessible

landscape for most small businesses and arts organizations, so having a small, independent media outlet on their side who can help get the word out about their organization or event can be a very attractive prospect. For you, the radio station owner, the value comes in the exposure to a diversity of audiences. Becoming a media partner for a small theatre festival in your area is win/win for both you and the festival, since they are getting the word out about their event, and you are getting exposure to their audiences, who all have the potential to be long-term listeners. While media partnerships could, eventually, turn into a moneymaking strategy for your station, don't dismiss the purely promotional value, not to mention experience, you stand to gain by doing it for free. Media partnerships usually take lots of time and hard work (which is why I saved it for last) but can be a goldmine when it comes to promoting your station.

Final thoughts

My intention in writing this book has been to provide you with a "soup-to-nuts" approach to imagining, building, and promoting a 24/7 live Internet radio station, and I hope that you have found much of the information valuable. As I said at the beginning, my goal was to write the guide I wish I'd had when starting out, and I hope that's what I've given you. Nothing in this book is easy, and the most important ingredient is something I cannot provide you - a passion for doing what you love. If you've got that, then you're halfway there, and I hope this book helps you the rest of the way. I would truly love to hear any success stories based on the techniques I've given you in this book, so please feel free to email me at tom@ radiofreebrooklyn.com and let me know where I can hear your station just as soon as you've launched. You may also email me with any questions about the material in this book at any point along the way. By the same token, if you find anything in this book inaccurate, outdated, or incomplete, I'd appreciate hearing that as well. I hope to do future editions of the book, and your input is extremely valuable. Be sure to sign up at http://www.radiocookbook.com in order to get a first look at future chapters and editions.

Now, do you feel ready? Good. GO MAKE RADIO!!

Appendix: Resources

Below, you will find a comprehensive listing of most of the resources mentioned in the book, along with several that are not. This list comprises resources you may find valuable in building your Internet radio station.

Websites About Digital Audio and Internet Radio:

- *Transom* (http://www.transom.org) - Transom is a fantastic resource for anyone interested in digital audio, including Internet radio and podcasting. The site features reviews and recommendations of audio gear, articles, interviews, tutorials, and tips on best practices.

- *The Prometheus Radio Project* (http://www.prometheus-radio.org) - The Prometheus Radio Project is an excellent "first stop" for anyone interested in getting into either low-power terrestrial radio or Internet streaming radio. Their site features articles, guides, and resources for those seeking to build community radio stations. Their stated goal is to "demystify technologies, the political process that governs access to our media system, and the effects of media on our lives and our communities."

- *Radio4all* (http://www.radio4all.net/) - Comprehensive directory of radio programming available for syndication

Stream Hosting Companies:

- *Internet-Radio.com* (http://www.internet-radio.com) - Stream hosting prices as low as $25 per month for 320kbps bitrate and 500GB bandwidth. Alternatively, select a pay-as-you-go plan, and only pay for the bandwidth you use. Their website also features a directory of streaming radio stations and an active user forum. Offers both SHOUTcast and Icecast servers.

- *Museter* (http://www.museter.com) - Prices start at $6.95 per month for 24kbps and 128kbps plans start at $32.95. All plans feature unlimited bandwidth and unlimited listeners. Offers both SHOUTcast and Icecast servers.

- *MyRadioStream* (http://www.myradiostream.com) - Provides free and low-cost stream hosting for bands, artists, community radio stations and DJs. SHOUTcast servers only.

- *ShoutCheap* (http://www.shoutcheap.com) - Prices start at $4.95 per month for 32kbps and 128kbps plans start at $11.95 for 25 listeners. Offers both SHOUTcast and Icecast servers.

- *Wohooo Networks* (http://www.wohooo.net) - Prices start at $15 per month for 64kbps and 128kbps plans start at $25 for 800 listeners. Offers both SHOUTcast and Icecast servers.

- *Centova Control Panel* (http://www.centova.com/en/cast) - Very popular control panel technology used by many stream host providers.

Radio Automation and Scheduling

- *MegaSeg* (http://www.megaseg.com) - Radio automation software for Mac OS.

- *RadioLogik* (http://www.macinmind.com/Radiologik) - Another radio automation software for Mac OS.

- *SAM Broadcaster* (http://spacial.com/sam-broadcaster) - Radio automation and broadcasting software for those using the Windows OS.

- *Prometheus Radio's Guide to Automation* (http://www.prometheusradio.org/sites/default/files/Automation_Handbook_color.pdf) - Excellent guide with case-studies to available automation technologies.

Software and Digital Tools:

- *Rogue Amoeba* (https://www.rogueamoeba.com/) - Creator of several invaluable audio tools for those using the Mac OS, including Nicecast and Audio Hijack (see chapter 5.)

- *butt* (http://butt.sourceforge.net/) - Free, easy to use, multi-platform broadcasting software.

- *IFTTT* (http://www.ifttt.com) - Free, web based engine that creates actions based on given conditions. Great for building your own automation systems (see chapter 5.)

- *Miro* (http://www.getmiro.com) - Open source music and video player that can be used to automatically download syndicated radio programs (see chapter 5.)

- *Hazel* (http://www.noodlesoft.com/hazel.php) - Inexpensive, effective automation system for Mac users. Required for many of the systems described in chapter 5.

- *Chrome Remote Desktop* (https://chrome.google.com/web-store/detail/chrome-remote-desktop/gbchcmhmhahfdph-khkmpfmihenigjmpp) - Free, easy to use remote desktop software that will allow you to log in to your studio computer from remote locations, including tablets and phones. An invaluable asset to any radio station.

WordPress and Website Resources:

- *WPBeginner* (http://www.wpbeginner.com/) - The largest free resource site for WordPress beginners.

- *WooCommerce* (http://www.woothemes.com/woocommerce/) - A free ecommerce toolkit for WordPress. Requires a payment gateway for credit card transactions.

- *Flagship Payment Gateway* (http://www.flagshipmerchant-services.com/) - A low cost, quality payment gateway for taking credit cards on your website.

WordPress Plugins Described in This Book:

- *Alligator Popup* (https://wordpress.org/plugins/alligator-popup/) - Allows you to enter a shortcode to add links to pages/posts which will be opened in a popup window. Useful for creating a popup audio player.

- *Auto Prune Posts* (https://wordpress.org/plugins/auto-prune-posts/) - Auto deletes posts or pages in a given category after a certain amount of time. Used for deleting "Now Playing" posts after they've been displayed on the home page

- *Redirection* (https://wordpress.org/plugins/redirection/) - Redirects web visitors from one page to another. Used as a convenient way to direct visitors who click on a "Now Playing" module to a show page instead of to the post.

- *MP3-jPlayer* (https://wordpress.org/plugins/mp3-jplayer/) - A WordPress audio player that supports both Icecast and SHOUTcast streams, and allows you to configure your own radio player for your website

- *Pods* (https://wordpress.org/plugins/pods/) – A free plugin used for creating custom content types in WordPress. Not as robust as WP-Types and Views, but effective nonetheless

- *Timetable Responsive Schedule For WordPress* (http://codecanyon.net/item/timetable-responsive-schedule-for-wordpress/7010836/) - A powerful and easy-to-use schedule plugin for WordPress. Great for helping you to create a weekly schedule for your website

- *Types* (http://www.wp-types.com) - Types defines content types in WordPress, including custom post types, custom taxonomy and Custom fields. A very powerful tool with a moderate learning curve.

- *Weekly Schedule* (https://wordpress.org/plugins/weekly-schedule/) - A free alternative to the Timetable plugin.

- *WP Latest Posts* (https://wordpress.org/plugins/wp-latest-posts/) – A very useful plugin for use in creating an automated "On Now" module on your website.

- *WP-Views* (https://wp-types.com/) - A companion plugin to Types, WP-Views allows you to display custom content in a variety of ways.

Content Distribution:

- *AudioBoom* (http://www.audioboom.com) - Audio content service that provides and excellent solution for hosting and distribution of your non-music radio shows.

- *iTunes Podcasts* (http://www.apple.com/itunes/podcasts/specs.html) - Apple's guide to submitting a podcast to the iTunes store.

- *Mixcloud* (http://www.mixcloud.com) - Excellent, free solution for hosting and sharing of your music radio shows. Features unlimited uploads and takes care of royalty fees for you. Highly recommended.

- *Stitcher* (http://www.stitcher.com) - Provides free distribution of your non-music radio shows via RSS to listeners using their popular mobile app.

- *TuneIn* (http://www.tunein.com) - TuneIn is a tremendously popular mobile radio app, and a great way to expand your listener based to millions of potential listeners.

Promotional Resources:

- *Printful* (http://theprintful.com) - Print-on-demand and fulfillment service featuring everything from t-shirts to mugs to throw pillows. Highly recommended.

- *PsPrint* (https://www.psprint.com/) - Printing service providing quality stickers at a reasonable price and very fast turnaround time.

- *Print Runner* (http://www.printrunner.com/) - Another sticker printing service with lower prices than PsPrint, but longer turnaround.

- *Vistaprint* (http://www.vistaprint.com) - A very popular online printing service with business cards starting at just $16.

- *MOO* (http://www.moo.com) - Another resource for business cards. Prices are slightly higher than VisaPrint, but quality, customer service, and turnaround time are all excellent.

- *Mailchimp* (http://www.mailchimp.com) -

- *Fiverr* (http://www.fiverr.com) - A marketplace of users providing a wide array of services from logo design to voiceovers, all at a single price point of just $5.

Books:

- *Radiotexte* by Bart Plantenga (http://www.amazon.com/Radiotext-E-Bart-Plantenga/dp/0936756942) - Incredible collection of historical writing about all things radio.

- *The Alternative Media Handbook* by Kate Coyner, Tony Dowmunt, and Alan Fountain (http://www.amazon.com/Alternative-Media-Handbook-Practice/dp/0415359651) - A "hands-on" guide to the practice of alternative media.

- *Radio Programming and Branding: The Ultimate Podcast-*

ing and Radio Branding Guide (http://www.amazon.com/Radio-Programming-Branding-Ultimate-Podcasting/dp/0692331492) - This book will help you improve your craft and effectively develop a winning brand that attracts attention, followership, and, ultimately, advertisers.

Made in the USA
Middletown, DE
10 August 2016